Guy Marks undertook his first serious
studies at Cirencester, he set off in a L;
from Calais to Cape Town.
On his return he spent several years in a convei...
becoming a commodity broker in the City of London.
Quitting that life in 1989, he became an overland tour leader working in Asia, the Middle East and South America.
He took up freelance travel writing and photography full-time in 1993 and has enjoyed success in this field. He has become a regular contributor to magazines and newspapers, as well as having his photographic work published in books, travel brochures and advertisements.
Guy Marks is a member of the British Guild of Travel Writers.

Travel Writing
and
Photography

All you need to know to make it pay

Guy Marks

Traveller's Press

First published in Great Britain in 1997 by
Traveller's Press
1 and 2 Cobbolds Row
Earl Soham
Suffolk IP13 7RL
Tel/Fax 01728 685894

British Library Cataloguing in Publication Data.
A catalogue record for this book is available from the British Library.

ISBN 0 9529271 0 1

Printed and bound in Great Britain by
The Ipswich Book Company Ltd, Ipswich, Suffolk IP3 9QR

Contents

Presenting the photographs: Physical presentation of slides p119, Image identification p125, Should slides be sent? p125, The illustrated article p127

Acknowledgements

I would like to extend my thanks to my wife Amanda, who has painstakingly appraised and edited my work, not just in the process of producing this book, but over the course of establishing myself as a travel writer and photographer.

I am most grateful to the many people who have helped me to complete this book, and in particular to Pat Yale for her information on guide book writing in chapter 3; to Lyn Hughes, Simon Calder, Nicholas Crane and Hilary Bradt for granting me the interviews in chapter 13, and to Kecia Harris for copy editing.

To free spirits

Preface

About three years ago I made the somewhat strange decision to become a travel writer and photographer. It was a new career to me and everything had to be learnt from scratch. I have no background in literature or journalism and had never attended a single lesson in photography.

Since that day two and a half years ago my work has taken me to some extraordinary destinations around the world. Each time my travel has been paid for, with the exception of the very first commission for which I had to pay my own air fare.

It is as hard for me to believe as it will be for you, but in this short time my work has taken me to Mexico, Guatemala, Belize, Honduras, Nicaragua, Costa Rica, Panama, Sudan, Eritrea, Ethiopia, Kenya, Holland, Belgium, France, Monaco, Italy, San Moreno, The Greek Islands, Austria, Switzerland, Germany and the Czech Republic.

I have already agreed to go to Alaska, Canada, seven states of the USA and back to Mexico before three years of this career are up. In the past month I have been in negotiations to travel on courtesy trips to Iran, Belize, Costa Rica, Madagascar, South Africa, Finland, Indonesia and the Northern Territory of Australia. By the time this book is completed I would expect at least one of these negotiations to come good.

In this time my work has appeared in The Financial Times, The Sunday Times, The Times, The Mail on Sunday, The Express, Wanderlust Magazine, The News and Travel Magazine (TNT), Independent & Specialist Travel Magazine, Trailfinders Magazine as well as in brochures, advertisements, public slide shows and the promotional publications of several travel companies. By the time the book is complete I hope to have cracked a few more of the broad-sheets and a couple more magazines.

Every single step of the way I seem to have done the wrong thing. I've upset travel editors of a number of publications, a couple of picture editors, and at least one major tour operator that could have been very useful to my career. It is my hope that this book will enable you to avoid the pitfalls into which I have inadvertently stumbled.

My first business year was supported by a tiny grant from a business enterprise scheme and I just about broke even, although my work included many hours of labour, painting the outside of pig sheds to supplement my income. In my second year there was no side-lining in whitewash or government hand-outs. I have every confidence that my third year will turn a reasonable profit.

More and more people are taking an interest in my work and more and more people want to know how it's done. It is perhaps because I am new to the business that I can still remember all the mistakes I have made along the way, and all the valuable and hard lessons I have learnt to make this a success. In fact much of it is still new to me and I'm learning as I go along.

Much of what I have to say is very simple and this book is certainly not aimed at anyone already making a living out of travel writing and photography although it may shed some fresh light on aspects of the industry they have taken for granted. What I would dearly like to do is to be able to convey the things I have found out over these past few years. It is fresh, basic and I hope understandable. All the help in the world can never replace experience, but being well informed can save a great deal of heartache and stress. If the information I give in the following pages had been available to me in a single source, I am sure that I would have made an even greater success far earlier.

Anyway I will let you be the judge of that. I will assume you know nothing of the subject as *I* didn't when I started. I hope you don't find the information patronising but if you do, you are probably way ahead of me!

You don't have to devote your whole life to this occupation as I have done, but if you even get one picture or a single article published as a result of the information in this book I will have fulfilled my intent and you at least will have covered the cost of the book. Good luck, and don't forget to let me know how you get on.

Chapter 1

Why travel writing *and* photography?

This is a book about travel writing and photography. Writing may be one skill and photography another but when it comes to the subject of travel, they go hand in hand. Open any newspaper or magazine and look at the travel articles. Nearly all of them will have photographs to illustrate them. Open any book on travel, be it a guide book or a book of travel literature and you will invariably find photographs. Some are heavily illustrated and others may have the photo pages as a small insert. Whatever the written content just about all of them will have a photo somewhere, even if it is only a single cover shot.

If you look at publications in which the photographs are the prime medium you will still find writing. Even the most visual of coffee-table picture books have short stories or sections of text. They may have whole pages describing what is going on in the pictures to put the visual expression into context, or they may have a foreword that introduces the reader to the main body of the photographic work. If nothing else the pictures will have a caption. The caption has to be written just as the photograph has to be taken.

A number of travel writers don't take pictures at all. They see it as a separate art and leave it up to the 'professional' photographers. When the article is written and accepted for publication, someone has to go to the trouble of finding some photographs to go with it. This is undertaken by a picture editor who has contacts with individual photographers and picture libraries. A lot of time and effort is put into finding the pictures and that means money is being spent. The pictures that are used are unlikely to have the exact visual impact that could have been achieved if a photographer had actually been there at the time standing next to the writer.

For this reason some writers form a working relationship with photographers. As a team they do indeed get the very best of both worlds; the professional photograph alongside the professional written word. This is not at all common though, because of the financial restraints. Many trips make very poor economical returns for a travel writer, even without having to support a photographer out of the proceeds.

An alternative is for the travel writer to take a few photos himself. These have the advantage of spontaneity and can very often compliment the text extremely well. It is not difficult to obtain a passable photograph with the hi-tech automatic cameras that are on the market today. I have heard many a writer say that it is always handy to have a few photos. Most of them consider their writing to be their profession and the photography as an aside. It is an extra, not taken seriously and sometimes even treated with contempt.

One well respected travel writer who has written a book on the subject told me "I know nothing about photography. I have a little automatic camera that I point and shoot and I seem to get some useable results. I only want a few pictures to illustrate an article and if I take a couple of rolls there is bound to be something good enough to use." Sure enough some quite ordinary pictures get published.

I was also surprised to hear similar comments about writing from the professional travel photographers. At a lecture about his work, the travel photographer Tom Owen Edmunds said "sometimes it is difficult to sell a photo on its own. It helps to have some words." He then held up a series of articles he had written. Each of the articles was drawn from the same experiences on a single trip. With rather amusing results he had skilfully tailored the words to the style of the particular publication for which it was intended. Whether sensationalised for the tabloids or made more down to earth for the broadsheets, each of the articles had enabled him to sell his pictures. I could only see the headlines from where I was sitting in the audience, so I have no idea what the quality of the text was like. He was quite dismissive about it, however, and certainly saw the words as an aside, despite his admirably successful ability to write such pieces.

Why travel writing **and** photography?

I suppose if you are an exceptional photographer you can sell your work on the basis of the photos and if the text is reasonable it will be accepted. Similarly if you are an exceptional writer your text will sell and the photos will be accepted. Isn't it a pity, though, to treat half of your productive output as an aside.

Imagine the potential of taking both parts of the job seriously. The *package* of photographs and text together by the same originator is highly desirable to publishers. It cuts down on time and money and quite simply it is complete and looks good. It is because it looks good that they use photographs and text together in their publications in the first place.

Some editors have told me that the availability of photographs is not a selling point for an article. The quality of the writing is all that matters and they can always find photos from a library. Well this might be true for some publications. Obviously if the article is complete rubbish the fact that there are photos with it will not make an editor accept it. Despite the opinions of those editors who have expressed opposing views, I can genuinely say that in my own experience the photos have contributed to selling my articles:

"Dear Guy.. I am interested in the white-water rafting piece, especially if you have good photographs. "- Paul Betts, Travel Editor, Weekend FT.

If there is a market for selling a colour photo to a newspaper that prints in black on pink paper then imagine how great a market there is for all the glossy colour magazines. Every newsagent's shelves are lined with highly illustrated magazines; in fact it is the illustrations that are the very first thing the eye sees when glancing along the shelf.

There is a picture on the front of a magazine which relates to a written feature known as the cover story. The front cover is selling the magazine and if the story is yours you should want the photo to be yours. The highest prices are paid for cover shots and it is heartbreaking if someone else is getting money for illustrating your story.

If you take both aspects seriously you have every chance of making your travels profitable. You don't have to limit yourself to taking photographs alone or writing articles alone. I always aim to return from a trip with words and pictures. Of course the ideal situation would be to sell both together, but there is no need to stop there. It is quite possible that some of the photos I take will suit more markets than just the one to accompany my articles, and some of the writing may not require illustration at all. By using every chance to sell the pictures on their own or the writing on its own I double my market.

Obviously it is a relatively simple point to apply the principle that if you double your product you double your income, but how you go about putting the principle into practice is not quite so simple. Finding those markets, selling to them and economically producing the writing and the photographs in the first place is the key to success. In fact I could write a whole book identifying the ways to make it pay!

Chapter 2

Raising money, travelling free

Travel costs money. Even if you travel around England or your local area you will run up bills. Trains, buses, boats, cars, horses, camels and aeroplanes all have their price. Then there are all the costs of accommodation be it a tent or a five-star hotel. To get the most out of the places you visit there are bound to be things you want to do that cost money. Every museum or site entrance fee, guide, day trip or city tour adds up to a considerable expense.

You might view the prospect of writing and photographing your travels as a means to cover those costs. The idea of free travel is very appealing and it is certainly possible. There is a vast difference, however, between covering costs and making travel pay. I accept that the main difference is an emphasis on money and that many travellers are free spirits who just want to see the world for the experience, and abhor the very concept of money. I will make no apologies, though, in making a big issue of the economics of travel. Money *does* make the world go round. On the one hand tourism has become the world's biggest industry, and on the other, travel is exclusive to those that can afford it; you certainly don't see the average citizen of a third world country saving up for his holiday in England....but I digress.

The point is, that if you want to make travel writing and photography pay, you will have to find ways not only to cover your costs but to end up with a profit. The degree to which you want to make it pay is a matter for your personal choice, but I aim to make a living out of it, and the tone of this book is aimed to that end. So we need to have a look at who holds the purse strings. Who has the authority to give away money or free travel? There are only two categories; the benevolent and the commercial. The benevolent are the organisations that do not want anything in return. The commercial are looking for some economic justification and viability for helping you with your plans.

Grants, awards and prizes.

There is a wealth of grant monies that can be tapped into for anyone who is really trying to make a go of things. The key is that you do have to be *really* trying. No one is going to give you money just for the asking. To that end, you have to be able to prove what you are doing, or intend to do, and indeed convince someone that you have the ability to carry out your plans. There *are* people that manage to abuse the system but that only makes it more difficult to persuade grant authorities that you are genuinely looking for help, not a handout.

There are different government controlled grants available in different areas. The schemes come and go and can even be politically motivated. I'm sure everyone realises that transferring someone from a dole queue to a 'scheme' takes them off the unemployment figure. The cost to the tax payer may be very similar. A scheme, however, may be seen as retraining or education with an ultimate purpose. That is something that most tax payers in our society are only too happy to encourage.

To find out about the schemes at any particular time in your area you can start at the job centre, the chamber of commerce, the citizens advice bureau and the arts council. My experience is that this leads to a long trail of people trying to block your way. If you fight through the red tape and take a pro-active attitude towards these schemes you may well find that you qualify for one of them.

I applied to the local Enterprise Centre who were running a programme on behalf of the local TEC (Training Enterprise Council). The programme was to help start up new businesses and included a small financial grant as well as practical training and advice on running a business.

I was turned down a couple of times before I'd even put in the forms, on the basis that they do not accept writers onto these schemes. Their reasoning was that someone may spend a year or so with no income while they write a book and then may or may not sell it, which makes it impossible to comply with the business forecasts and predictions - don't I know it!

I was not deterred, however, and pursued the matter with ever increasing anger at the implication that my business was not a 'proper' business. You can't work against these bureaucrats; you have to find a way to work with them. As soon as I mentioned that I was a photographer as well as a writer, which was just a chance comment, their whole attitude changed. Photographers could apply to the scheme even though writers could not. I produced a business plan with budgets and forecasts based entirely on supposition. It was enough to satisfy the authorities and I was taken on to the scheme.

This was a very minor triumph and the grant was minimal. It was, nevertheless, a grant; a benevolent contribution to my business for which I thank the tax payer. It meant that for the first year I had some money coming in every week. It was above board and I didn't have to pretend I was looking for a job and claim unemployment. I *had* a job - my own business.

At the very first business review the counsellor asked me if I was writing to travel or travelling to write. Of course the two are inextricably linked in this case which made the question unanswerable. It was typical of the whole system though, unanswerable questions from people who could no more understand the intricacies of my business than fly to the moon.

I can't say what grants will be available to any particular individual, but you should certainly check all avenues and not take no for an answer if you think you ought to qualify. If you can't find public money then you have to look for private money. It may come as a surprise to learn that there are dozens of awards and prizes given away every year. Many of these are to promote writing and photography for its own sake. Some are given by trusts which have been set up to commemorate various individuals whose names they bare. Others are run by societies to promote their genre. Large companies also sponsor some of the awards, which is more a commercial than benevolent attitude; they are doing it as a form of advertising and PR to raise the public awareness of their company name or product.

Most of these awards are advertised in the newspapers and in specialist magazines on writing and photography. There are also publications which list all the major ones. *The Writer's Handbook* published annually by Macmillan and the *Writers' & Artists' Yearbook* published annually by A&C Black both have extensive sections on this subject. They list all the organisations that have regular awards but it is worth looking out for the one-off awards.

When it comes to photographic awards and prizes I haven't found any publications that list them all in one place. The individual awards are often advertised in the photography magazines that you find on the shelves of any high street newsagents. The prizes are used as selling points for many magazines. Everybody wants to have a competition and it seems the camera manufacturers and suppliers are often happy to sponsor the competition. In general, however, they tend to be giving away their latest product as the main prize. These can be quite substantial products but not necessarily something you need at that particular moment. Just by the fact that you have won a photographic competition it is clear that you already have an adequate camera!

It would be a mistake to base your business on getting one of these awards as the competition is fierce and ultimately you either have to be the best, or very lucky. Having said that, it is well worth being aware of the awards and prizes as a potential source of extra support for your projects and the kudos of having won something will stand you in good stead. I go into a little more detail of the importance of kudos and getting yourself known in chapter 8.

Press trips

Press trips are run to all sorts of exotic locations by those who have an interest in publicising the destination or the actual travel itself. These are invariably free of charge even including flights, accommodation, excursions and just about anything you could want.

Raising money, travelling free

It sounds idyllic, but who runs them and how do you get onto them?

They are run by tourist boards, PR companies, airlines and tour operators. Frequently there is a cooperation between such organisations to put together a trip. For example a tourist board will put a package together with the help of an airline and a tour operator. Together they can fly you off and cart you around their particular destination to give you a taste of what it has to offer. It's a great idea for all concerned. The "press" member gets to see all the best places for free and doesn't have to put much effort into organising his trip, and the promotional organisation hopes to get press coverage.

The best possible advertising is editorial with the writer praising the company or the destination. If you look in most publications you will find a note at the end of the articles that says the writer travelled with ... or travelled courtesy of ... This could well mean that the writer was given a free trip although this is not always the case. There is no real way to distinguish between company names given for information or mentioned because they gave a free trip.

Press trips are a commercial venture and there does need to be some kind of justification for getting a place on these trips. Even when the trip is run by a country's tourist board out of tax payers' money, the promotion is still for commercial gain.

It is far more difficult for a freelance to get onto these trips than it is for a staff writer. If a staff writer goes there is almost a guarantee that an article about the trip will get published. The freelance finds it much more difficult to make any guarantees.

The organisers' concerns are perhaps unfounded, as a freelance is quite likely to write several articles about the trip because this is the only way he can make it pay. If you spend a week or ten days travelling and then spend time actually writing about it when you get back, a single article will simply not provide a living. This means that there is every chance that the subject of the press trip will get published in a number of different places all from one author. The staff writer, on the other hand, will probably only publish in his own particular publication.

This play-off between guarantees and potential scope of cover is something that only the organisers of the press trip can decide. What normally happens is that you are offered the press trip only if you can get a commission in a suitable publication. Having got your commission you will be welcomed onto the trip with open arms. Have a look at the section on getting commissions in chapter 9 to see how to go about this.

There are a few disadvantages to press trips. Normally they run with several press members on the same trip. Many potential trip members will have been approached and competition to get onto the trip is high. Editors at the top outlets for travel articles will therefore be approached by several freelance writers, all with the same idea. They may even have been approached directly by the trip organisers offering free trips for them, or a member of their staff. This really doesn't make it easy to sell a piece. Originality is so important that over-sell can kill an idea even before the travel has begun.

If you do get on the trip and have your one commission in hand, you will find you are not alone. The other press members on the trip will also want to write articles about exactly the same things and will be submitting to the same editors on their return.

Press trips can also be a little restrictive in that you only get a chance to see what the organisers want you to see. This will obviously be all the good things about a place, which is great, but a little unbalanced. The trip could be conducted at such a pace that there just isn't time to go off on your own and find out the things you want to know about a place. You could easily be force-fed on a diet of hype and PR. This is not necessarily a problem, as long as you use your own judgement about the situation. It is quite a privileged and enviable experience to have people showing you all the good things.

To get any respect for our work it is important that readers feel they are not being led astray. Press trip organisers do take a calculated chance and you are under no obligation to write good things about the trip. In fact quite the opposite is true; you are morally obliged to tell it how it is.

Tailor-made trips

In addition to press trips, many of the organisations I have mentioned in the above paragraphs are quite happy to organise individual trips for you.

Some of the most forward thinking tour operators are only too happy to get writers onto their trips. The same reasoning applies to their generosity; if you go on their trips you will write about them. The actual deal you can get depends on your ability to sell yourself and convince the organisation of the degree to which giving you a trip will be to their benefit.

In these situations it is far more a question of individual initiative than being part of a group invited to an organised event. What you need here is to have an idea, get a commission, and then approach the organisations to see who will or won't help with your travel arrangements. It might be that someone will pick up your entire bill or it could be that they will just provide part of what you need. Every little helps, though, and every opportunity should be considered.

A tour company might give you the trip without flights - it may cost them very little to give you unsold space on a trip. You can then approach an airline to see if they will help with the flights. They, in turn, may not wish to give too much away, but might at least give you a cost price flight as opposed to standard rate. So at the end of the day you get all your travel but have only paid for a cut price flight. It's not ideal but already a lot better than having to pay for everything yourself. Any reduction in costs has to be a good thing and it really is the only way to make this business pay.

We do have to remember that we are not actually *entitled* to free travel just because we write about it and photograph it. The people in charge of the purse strings must get extremely fed up with would-be writers and photographers looking for freebies. It really does have to be mutually beneficial and it is worth thinking about their point of view; only ask for something that will cost them little or nothing but is worth a great deal to you. In the early days when you are not known and can't get commissions it might be that you have to pay for all of your travel and indeed this won't pay. It is a business and to set up any business you have to make investments. Perhaps your first trips won't pay, but if you get published as a result of them it will all help to further your career.

Getting free trips can be done though, and there are tour operators that are delighted just to get people on their trips. I recently interviewed one of the directors of a tour company for an article that was published in the AITO Outlook (a newsletter sent to members of AITO - the Association of Independent Tour Operators). The director had this to say:

"Maybe I'm naive, but I think that if you really feel you've got a good product you shouldn't be scared of getting the journalists on the trip."

That is just the sort of attitude that has brought his company no end of publicity and I'm sure his comments will be well received by other operators within the association. It does illustrate quite clearly that tour operators do actually want us on their trips.

I know he has taken people on trips when they haven't actually had pre-arranged commissions. Some of the resultant articles, even from staff writers, have taken the best part of a year to appear in print and some have never actually appeared at all. It has made him far more discerning about who he takes, and quite rightly too. There are people that just con free travel out of trusting operators and their antics taint people's attitudes, making it more difficult for the rest of us.

Even so, we must not lose sight of the ethics of taking free trips as I mentioned before. The key words in the above quote were "If... you have got a good product". If, of course, the operator hasn't got a good product no amount of free trips should get him good publicity. The opinions of their product, or the place that was visited, should always remain unbiased even if it means criticising someone who has provided travel facilities.

Paid commissions

In chapter 9 on proposals and commissions I look into the detail of how to go about writing proposals in order to get commissions from magazine and newspaper editors. That type of commission refers to an agreement to take and pay for a finished piece of work, as opposed to being paid to go and do something which is what I am referring to below.

Obviously staff writers get all their travel paid for by the publication for which they work. As a freelance you may think it is impossible to get paid to go travelling but this is not the case.

Commissioning editors, particularly for books, often have a budget to get a particular piece of work done for their publication.

Guide book publishers are perhaps a prime example. They want a section of a book to be researched and written, and want someone competent to go and do it. They usually agree a fixed fee for the work which is not dependent on sales of the book. Rather than claiming expenses from the book publisher you simply get the work done and pay for everything out of the money given to you. The balance is your payment, so it is in your interest to do things as cheaply as possible. The difficulty is that some of the budgets offered are impractical and not even workable. If you don't know what it is going to cost you, and how long it will take to complete the commission, it puts you in a very difficult position to negotiate a fixed fee. You could end up with what seemed like a good idea actually costing you money, and effectively you are subsidising the publisher.

Publishers aren't out to con you but it could be that they have a different idea from yours. You need to establish your expectations right at the start. Some people are happy to go and do this work just for the experience and the travel and so don't actually expect to make money from it.

You might want to work out the budget with the publisher so that they know what you are expecting to spend. Then if there are extraordinary unforeseen costs you will be able to approach them and confirm that these costs were not budgeted for. They may then be able to pay the extra, but you must know where you stand before you take on these commissions.

If you have been paid to go and do a specific piece of work, it does not usually preclude you from doing other work while you are there. You often see articles that have a note about the writer that says they have just completed updating or writing a guide book on the area. This way you have your free or paid travel for the commission but still sell articles about the trip on a freelance basis.

If you are a writer *and* photographer there is an even greater opportunity for this kind of paid commission. There are a whole host of people who want places or things photographed and they are prepared to pay to get a professional to do it. Of course you are up against amateur photographers who will go for nothing and even professionals who see the job as a bit of free travel - an excellent way to get their holiday for free.

When the subject matter to be photographed is of a specialist nature the photo researchers will not find exactly what they want lurking in the files of slide libraries. This is when they commission a professional to go and get the right photos. This could be to get photographs for a book, a brochure or advertising material to promote a particular product.

Anyone who is running a trip to a new destination for the first time will not have any photos for their promotions. They may not want to rely on the chance that the trip leader or one of the customers brings back the right thing, so they send a photographer on the trip. Obviously your first obligation is to get the photographs that you have been paid to get, but that doesn't stop you taking extra photos.

You have to make sure the commissioning company is happy with the arrangement, but they can easily see that if they want you full time, and exclusivity on all the pictures you take whilst on the trip, it will cost them a lot more money. They would have to pay full photographic fees. According to the NUJ these range from £130 for the national newspapers day rate, to in excess of six hundred pounds a day for "location work". Travelling to take the photos in a particular place would surely be classified as location work.

Before you get your hopes up I would have to say that this is simply not the travel writer and photographer's league, and commissioning companies don't have this sort of money. The longest photographic commission I've done so far lasted for nine weeks - imagine that on a rate of £600 per day - no, nor can I!

It is possible to get paid a reasonable sum for these commissions while being able to take lots of photos that you can sell elsewhere. You are also getting the travel experience and can take the opportunity to write lots of articles and illustrate them with your photos.

Raising money, travelling free

Whether you end up on a press trip, a tailor-made trip or a paid commission it is absolutely essential to write articles and to get them sold when you return. As I mentioned before, you need to sell more than one piece about the trip. If you are a travel writer and photographer you have the advantage over the others on the trip in that you can supply a finished piece to the editors. An illustrated article will sell far better and indeed will return much needed extra revenue. There might be articles that do not require photographs, but don't forget to look for markets for the photographs as well as the words. Any trip should yield some interesting shots. If you are working with a slide library there should be something to offer them when you get back. It is important to look for all these outlets because that is the only way to make it pay. There is no point in getting the free travel if you don't follow it up with a product that you can sell for cash. A free trip helps cut the costs but selling the results is the whole point of the business. You need to have several things going at a time. Even better than a free trip is the opportunity to get paid to go travelling, and come back with a product to sell.

One word of warning though; you will not succeed in this business if you see it just as a way to get free travel. You do have to be able to supply that product at the end of the day and you will be competing with other professionals in the industry. You have to have a real commitment and involvement in what you are doing. To quote Paul Gogarty, freelance writer and photographer, broadcaster and chief travel writer for the Daily and Sunday Telegraph: "You have to have a passion for travel and a passion for writing."

Chapter 3

Markets for travel writing

Having established in previous pages that travel writing and travel photography go hand in hand I want to look at the different markets in more detail. The ideal situation is to sell the two products together but there will be some markets that are word-led and others that are picture-led. The next two chapters deal with these markets in turn but it should always be remembered that the words need pictures and the pictures need words.

Newspapers

Perhaps the market that most obviously springs to mind for travel articles is that of the newspapers. The national papers invariably have a specific travel section within their pages, which typically appears at the weekend. There is a tendency to think of the Sunday papers as the ones with all those specialist sections but increasingly the Saturday papers are the ones with long travel sections.

Some of these papers rely on freelance contributions to get their material each week whilst others have teams of staff writers. It is sometimes quite difficult to distinguish between the two, even when you study the papers regularly. At some of the newspapers the chief travel writer is, in fact, freelance. The Sunday Times and the Saturday Telegraph both have freelance chief travel correspondents.

The great thing about newspapers is that they come out every day and have a travel section at least once a week. Those pages have to be filled and they certainly provide a market for the product we are looking at. Many magazines come out monthly or even quarterly which means that they simply don't use the quantity of articles that a newspaper does.

Having said that, it does not necessarily follow that just because the paper uses freelance contributors there are opportunities for every freelance writer. In fact it can be quite the opposite.

Everyone who is trying to start up thinks of the national papers and as a result the editorial departments get inundated with unsolicited manuscripts. These may be welcome but the quantity of submissions alone can mean that chances are slim. It also means that there is very little chance of getting through to the editors on the phone and even conversations with others within the department can be short and sweet. The actual number of national papers is also quite slim. How many are there to choose from that are accepting freelance work? I can't go into great depth on every paper, but the following selection shows the sort of response you can expect.

The Sunday Times have two writers that travel for them full time. Mark Ottaway is on staff and David Wickers is on contract. The travel editor Christine Walker and deputy travel editor Rob Ryan obviously have their input. There is also what they describe as a "*coterie of names in orbit*". That is to say there is a core of about a dozen known first choice freelance writers that submit ideas and write the majority of the editorial. The team tends to plan things about a year in advance, meeting and blocking out topics for the following year.

This ensures that they do not have to depend on the vagaries of what articles come in, but it does rather limit the potential for the newcomers. Having said that, this degree of planning does mean that a great deal of the work is being commissioned and some of this will be supplied by people who they have not published before. Things do get submitted that catch their eye, and do indeed get published.

Rob Ryan tells me that there is a tendency for people to send in things that are inappropriate and have no context to what The Sunday Times are doing. They may send in something which is a good story and has come about as a little vignette of part of their trip-of-a-lifetime. The problem is that it just isn't what people want to read about (at least in The Sunday Times pages). The things that catch the eye are the pieces which are not only well written but which are also tailor-made for The Sunday Times.

Timing is also a problem as people sometimes send in excellent articles but they are on a subject that has just been run, and so the paper won't want to cover it again for at least another year.

They do claim to read absolutely everything and to encourage good work when they see it. They welcome unsolicited manuscripts but you have to be aware of the limited chance of success. There are no hard and fast rules and it is nice to know that it is not a completely closed shop. Things do 'get through' all the time.

The Times has a travel section on a Saturday and on a Thursday. They seem a little less willing to discuss what opportunities there are for freelance writers but you only have to look through their pages to work it out. There are dozens of different contributors, most of whom only get the occasional piece published here. Then there are a few well-known established names that get several pieces in over a period of just a few months. It is clear that lots of the contributors are freelance and there are perhaps greater opportunities here than in The Sunday Times.

To give you an idea of the sort of reception you might get from an editorial department, I gave them a call, asked about freelance contributions, and was told: *"Just send them in for the attention of Brian MacArthur and I'm sure he will get back to you."* Brian MacArthur is the travel editor with responsibility for both the Saturday and the Thursday sections.

The Observer is perhaps the newspaper with the least opportunities for new writers. The travel editor Desmond Balmer heads the team and writes many of the articles himself. Some of the pieces that are published do come from freelance writers but it is rare that these will come from 'outside' contributors. *"The people we use are the ones we have used for a while and are on our established list,"* they told me, *"but don't let me stop you from sending something in if you really feel it might be of interest."*

The Guardian's travel editorial department is headed by travel editor Jeannette Page. She does take a few freelance contributions but points out that she needs so few that she can afford to be extremely selective.

The Independent has a lot of travel coverage but a large percentage of it is provided by the staff travel correspondent and editor Simon Calder. At present he has a Saturday section in the 'Weekend' and a section on a Wednesday. The **Independent on Sunday** has travel pages in the 'Review' and I have even noticed pieces by the travel editor in 'section two' of the Friday issue. Whilst there is increasing pressure for the staff writers to do all the work, there is only so much they can do in one lifetime. *"I do a lot of work, but they do give me some budget to buy things in. I can't do everything"* says Simon Calder. There are certainly opportunities here for freelance contributions and submissions are welcome, with the proviso that the article is not based around any free trips.

Simon Calder gives some advice and more details about The Independent in Chapter 13.

The Daily Telegraph at present has the biggest travel section of all the broadsheet newspapers and relies almost entirely on freelance material. Travel editor Gill Charlton not only looks after this huge travel section on Saturdays, but is also responsible for the section in **The Sunday Telegraph**. The chief travel writer is Paul Gogarty, who is in fact freelance, and there is a core of well known established writers that provide much of the copy. Having said that, the sheer volume of articles they use means there is always room for new talent. They do accept unsolicited manuscripts and generally respond fairly quickly. Gill Charlton has even taken the trouble to give me a few pointers when articles have not been suitable for her.

I think we can establish the trend from these newspapers; the norm is to have a core of writers, be they staff or freelance. Without exception, though, the chance of a newcomer sending in an unsolicited manuscript and getting it published may be small but it does exist, and there are actually quite a number of opportunities at some of the papers. I haven't gone into detail about them here, but don't forget all the other nationals like **The Financial Times**, **The Mail on Sunday** etc. Complete listings can be found in publications like *The Writer's Handbook* (Macmillan).

Perhaps the most important thing about these national newspapers is that they pay a reasonable price for the work they use. There are freelance rates recommended by the National Union of Journalists, but these are only guidelines and the papers can, and do, pay whatever they choose. Some papers pay higher rates than the NUJ minimums and this can be quite lucrative, but how frequently are you going to get articles published by them? The Independent make no bones about the fact that they are not great payers, but this is only in comparison with the other nationals. It will become clear in other sections of this book that money is not the only consideration in this business. Getting published in the nationals gives you considerable exposure to a very wide audience. Other people within the industry will see your name in print and this will certainly give you a foot in the door. It is a section of the market that really has to be approached, but there is little chance of making a living from the national papers alone. If all you ever do is attempt to get into this part of the market you will probably fail, having become completely despondent with piles of rejection letters. I regard getting something into the nationals as a minor triumph. It is a bonus rather than my bread and butter.

Regional Newspapers

Many regional newspapers have a travel section that runs once a week. This is often in their Saturday issue, just like the national papers.

Local papers don't have very much money and often rely on all their copy coming from staff writers or being sent in from readers. Sarah Hardy, travel editor of the Eastern Daily Press which has the largest circulation of all regional newspapers in the country, told me that she either writes the travel section herself or finds that staff at the paper are happy to write about their holiday. If the staff get their piece published they receive the princely sum of £30. As a travel writer you aren't going to make a living out of that, but in the early stages it is important not to dismiss any market.

This might be a way to get started if you are happy just to see your work in print. Getting things published is all part of the slog of getting established.

All you need to know about copyright

Here are the basics for copyright of words, and in particular for articles - see the next chapter for copyright of photos.

When you write something you own the copyright. You do not have to register it anywhere to be given that copyright. It is intrinsically yours. You can stake your claim to the words by writing the word 'copyright' or the © symbol and your name . This is usually followed by a date indicating when you wrote it. If somebody can prove they wrote exactly the same piece at an earlier date you are in trouble.

When you sell your written work to somebody for publication you do not necessarily sell the piece outright. What you are selling is the right for that publication to use the words in a certain way.

The normal standard that is used with UK publications such as newspapers and magazines is known as First British Serial Rights. This means that they are buying the right to be the first publication to print or serialise your work for publication within Britain.

After they have exercised this right and published your work you could still sell the piece again for publication in Britain, as long as the buyer is aware that it has previously been published. This would be known as Second British Serial Rights. A third sale for the same piece would be Third British Serial Rights, and so on. Better still, you can be more specific. If you know a publication only has a limited distribution you can limit the rights you are selling. Say a magazine is only printed and distributed in Suffolk; you could sell First Suffolk Serial Rights and then sell the same piece to someone in Gloucestershire with First Gloucestershire Serial Rights.

The rest of the world is still an open market. You have every right to sell the piece again with, say, First American Serial Rights to a publication in America.

You do have to be specific and make sure the buyer knows what you are selling him. If somebody thinks they have bought world rights and finds you have sold the piece elsewhere there will be nothing but aggravation even if you are technically correct.

If you are on the staff for someone as a writer, they may have the copyright to anything you produce, even if it is written in your spare time. This has to be checked in your contract of employment.

The rights sold when you sell a book to a publisher are far more complex. Every contract is different and you should seek professional advice before signing anything away.

__Magazines__

Perhaps the biggest market of all is the magazine market. Believe it or not there are around thirty national newspapers even though you might only be able to think of half a dozen you could contribute to. There are around a further one hundred publications when you look at the regional newspapers. But there are literally thousands of publications when it comes to magazines.

You can find listings of all the titles and publishers in books like *The Writer's Handbook* and there is even a book called *1000 Markets for Freelance Writers*. In actual fact the figure of 3000 consumer magazines and journals is commonly bandied about.

These are not all travel magazines and you could probably count the number of purely travel publications on one hand. Holiday and travel magazines frequently come on the market and disappear again after a few issues or a few years. If you are interested enough in travel writing and photography to have bought this book, then you probably already know which are the current and the best travel magazines.

Traveller is an established magazine which is published just four times a year and runs about six features per issue. It is of a very high standard and usually requires photographs to be submitted with the piece. They accept unsolicited manuscripts but have quite strict guidelines for contributors. These can be obtained from the editor Miranda Haines.

Independent and Specialist Travel has been going for about a year and comes out every second month. The editor Rebecca Pugh makes a strong point of having contributions from non-professional writers. They have a set of contributors guidelines and emphasise that they like a complete package including photographs. Rebecca welcomes ideas and unsolicited manuscripts.

Wanderlust is currently published every two months and there are good opportunities here. They accept freelance contributions from new writers as well as from established professionals. A copy of their guidelines can be obtained from the editorial office if you send an s.a.e. Lyn Hughes, the editor of Wanderlust, gives us her thoughts about getting into the industry in chapter 13.

There are other magazines such as **Business Traveller** (editor Gill Upton) which *are* purely travel, but they have an added speciality rather than a general travel appeal. All in all the purely travel based magazines are few and far between.

What about the rest of the 3000 publications? Obviously there are too many to discuss in detail, and they are not all going to have travel sections, but you would be surprised how many of them do. Even those that don't have a travel section per se will often be interested in stories from around the world that relate to their specialist subject.

Travel is a very broad ranging topic. The broader the view you take of what is or isn't a travel piece, the greater are the opportunities to find a suitable market. What you need to do on your travels is always to be looking for an angle, looking for something to write about. On each and every day when you are travelling there are dozens of things going on around you. Any one of them could be picked up on and made into a travel related article. The markets could well be specialist magazines which have a theme other than travel, but by tapping into these markets we can start to turn a profit.

For example: I was in a campsite in Alaska recently on a day when nothing much happened, or so it would seem at first glance.

The morning had been spent driving to Fairbanks from Denali National Park. We arrived in the campsite at around lunchtime and had a free afternoon to look around the area. I spent much of the afternoon in the campsite trying to do some writing on my laptop as well as venturing into town. Now that might sound like a fairly uneventful day but there is always something to write about.

The most obvious article to come out of this would be something about Denali National Park. You can imagine the sort of piece - wide open spaces, national parks full of bears, all the classic images of Alaska. You might think of The Independent as your market for this kind of travel piece. Well don't bother. Everyone who goes to Alaska writes about the wildlife and sends the piece in to The Independent they tell me. Of course that doesn't mean there isn't a piece to be written along these lines. If you live in a rural area there is probably a county magazine which has a travel section - you can bet they don't get many articles sent in about Alaska.

Having written the obvious article, look for the unusual. I said I spent some time using my laptop. Perhaps a computer magazine would be interested in the fact that a laptop is being used in a campsite in Alaska. That is fairly unusual and could make a good piece. There are hundreds of computer magazines and even the manufacturer of the laptop produces a customer magazine.

Then there is the campsite. It was an American site, so it was full of RVs. What is an RV? It's a recreational vehicle, what you and I would call a mobile home or motor caravan. You could write about these and offer the piece to a caravanning or camping magazine - again, there *are* such special interest publications.

A convention of Airstream caravans was also staying at the camp. These are the bright silver caravans that are quite streamlined and distinctive, and look like a cross between the space age and 1950s design, sort of '*Lost in Space*' technology. If you remember the kids' programme by that name you will know what I mean. Again this could have made an interesting article for caravan buffs or an amusing article for caravan haters - you just have to pick your market.

In the evening the local classic car club drove into the camp. They do this every Thursday night and stop for a chat with the campers. They came in old Dodges, Chevies and Fords and one of them even had an old Mini. Could this be an article for a classic car magazine?

The old boy driving a Model T Ford was quite a character. He claimed to have been the first person to drive up the Alaska Highway when it was first opened. This was quite a big event in the history of the area, not least because of the remarkable engineering feat that was achieved in building the road. For many Americans this was like the final frontier being opened. The man carried an old leather wallet that had an inscription commemorating the event. A couple of articles could come out of this - a historic piece on the Alaskan Highway and a factual piece on the survival of the old Model T Ford.

These are all incidental things that happened around me just in the campsite, and that's not including all the things that could be written about in town such as lifestyle pieces, American architecture, fast food, shopping malls, town planning based on everyone having a car and no thought about pedestrians - the opportunities were endless. My point is that there is always something to write about. It is no good just writing the conventional cliched travel pieces and hoping to find a market for them. Nor is it any use sending in the wrong sort of piece to a magazine. Having decided to write a piece on some obscure specialist topic you have to research that particular market. I don't know the ins and outs of the different magazines catering for caravaners, but if I were to write the pieces I mentioned above, I would have to find out. Research is half the battle. Having decided to write the piece it would be necessary to find out the style and format of the targeted publication in order to write the story and have a chance of it selling.

You may not consider this sort of piece to be a travel piece and perhaps it is not what you want to write about. It is difficult to make money from the travel pieces alone, however, and this sort of broad outlook will help to make your travels pay.

Airline Magazines

Every airline has its own in-flight magazine. Crammed in between the adverts, the duty free shopping lists and the details of the entertainment programmes are a number of travel articles.

Some of the ones that seem to get published are not of a particularly high standard whilst others are superb. I suspect they are sometimes provided by people whose first language is not English. Invariably there is an English translation somewhere in the magazine and in fairness perhaps the quality has been lost in the translation.

If they are bilingual magazines there is no reason why the editor shouldn't accept a manuscript in English and translate it into the local language just as readily as translating to English from the local language.

This can be an extremely lucrative market as part of your overall selling strategy. When you sell an article to a UK publication it is normal to sell just the First British Serial Rights. This still leaves the rest of the world as an open market for that exact same article. The airlines are often happy to buy publication rights for their particular area of operation and are not particularly bothered about the fact that it has been previously published in a different part of the world. They would normally buy rights for the country or area where the magazine is published, or if it is published in Britain they may well be happy to buy second or third rights. Selling an article more than once is a major step towards profitability.

It is important to do some research and find out what sort of thing they like to publish. You can usually get hold of a copy from the airline office.

One thing to note is that they tend only to print articles on destinations that they actually fly to. There is always a map showing their routes in the magazine somewhere so it doesn't take a great deal of research to work this out.

Don't be fooled into only thinking of your outward journey. If you are flying to Egypt you might expect to read something about Egypt in the in-flight magazine. What about all the Egyptians that have just got off the plane where you got on - wouldn't they like to read something about England?

Without doing any international travel at all you could probably supply half the airlines in the world with features on Britain. We have the busiest airports and all the major airlines come here, along with many of the smaller ones. What is more, they might all buy the same piece with rights to different areas.

Advertorial

This is a very grey area of travel writing. It is the merging of editorial and advertisement. There is nothing that gives better publicity to a product than an article which not only mentions it but gives it high praise. Marketing departments of companies realise this.

When the piece is printed it appears in the same style as the normal editorial for that particular publication. There might well be the word 'Advertisement' printed at the top of the article so that no one is being deceived, but the very fact that it is written in the style of the editorial will mean that some people will not realise that it is an advert and will take it as an unbiased report.

If you are an advertisement copy writer this way of making a living will come quite naturally. Unfortunately advertisement writers and travel writers don't quite come up with the same sort of editorial. The more the piece looks like editorial, the better it is for all concerned. There is therefore a vested interest in a company actually getting a travel writer to pen these pieces for them. The company rather than the publication is commissioning the piece and paying the writer.

There is obviously some question of ethics that arises from this type of writing. However, if you are just starting out, I can see no reason to overlook the advertorial market. Not only will someone pay you to write the piece, but also there is a guarantee of getting it published. Anything published helps your own cause and increases your exposure. In fact it is even worth doing it for nothing if you are going to get into print.

I have had experience of this and have indeed provided an article for a company free of charge. They knew that I would have something suitable about travelling with them that would show them in a good light. They paid for the space in the publication and I provided the article. I was absolutely amazed how many people saw that article and commented on it. None of them ever even suspected that the company I had mentioned in the piece had paid for the space or that I had not received a penny for my work.

In my book (and this *is* my book!) this was legitimate self-promotion. My motivation was for self publicity rather than to promote the tour operator, but we both did well out of it.

Sometimes an article will quite naturally mention a product or recommend something. You are not necessarily endorsing the company but there is no reason why you should not recommend something that you have found to be good. You may have been provided with services for free or at a discounted price, but that shouldn't and doesn't prohibit you from writing about them and saying they were good if you found that to be the case.

The more you think this through the more you find that there are no definite lines to say what is or isn't advertising, what is endorsement and what is reportage. This is why I began by saying that the whole issue is a grey area.

You can't argue with anyone who takes the moral high ground; they are right. You must use your own judgement and draw your own lines. Business is business and before you turn anything down you have to consider the benefits. If this is your mainstay, however, perhaps you should consider joining an advertising agency rather than becoming a travel writer.

Travel literature

The bookshop shelves are packed with hundreds of titles that are loosely classified as Travel Literature. They are, in general, books which people have written about their own travels. It is a massive market but an extremely competitive area.

In the early nineties the publishing industry, like just about everything else in Britain, fell into recession. Every book by a new and unknown author is a great financial risk to a publisher and travel literature was hit quite hard. The publishers made very sensible decisions that they would only consider publishing books that were virtually a dead certainty to sell. It's a wonderfully sensible attitude in business, but not much good if you happen to be an unknown writer trying to get into the business. The long term effect of this stance is that many would-be travel writers never got off the ground and, horror of horrors, probably had to chuck it all in and get a job.

The reading public was denied the choice to buy a travel book written by someone new. Instead there was a steady diet of travel books by personalities. These often accompany TV series and didn't necessarily make good travel reading. I think the theory must be that if a series is popular on television people will buy the book just out of familiarity. I'm sure these often end up as gifts: old uncle Fred enjoyed that on the telly so I can get him the book for Christmas. Of course I'm not suggesting that these books weren't every bit as good as the television programmes they accompanied, but this kind of exposure is very different from publishing a book by an unknown. The very nature of it means that you already have to be a known personality before your book is published.

Then there were a mass of old classic travel books re-published. Again they were dead-certs. Written by travel writers who had become household names, they provided the backbone of many a publisher's list. If you put a new cover on something and bring it out in paperback there are those who will recognise the author's name and might buy something that they don't even realise was written thirty or forty years ago.

The plus side of this is that if you can get published you might find your own works still bringing in the royalties in forty years' time!

Then there were the current contemporary writers that had had a book published in the latter half of the eighties. If their books had been successful they were called upon to write another. They were the only people that were actually getting commissions to go out and write new work, specifically for the travel literature market. This is not intended as a criticism, merely a statement of the market as I saw it a few years ago - low risk publishing which has paid off and kept the publishing houses in business.

Quite apart from the recession, it was generally accepted that travel was a declining literary area. It is something that comes and goes in trends although I wouldn't like to say whether or not this is led by the consumers not buying the travel books, or by the publishers not printing them and therefore not giving the consumer the choice.

My own research in the early nineties showed that out of 25 different publishers contacted, only a few were even prepared to listen to a proposal. Still fewer would read a synopsis and only a couple actually wanted to see a sample.

Rejections were coming through not on the basis that the idea or the book itself wasn't of a suitable standard, but simply because the publishers wouldn't consider anything on travel.

Here are a few of the comments I received along with the rejections three years ago:

"Travel-writing is a very competitive area of the market;" - Harper Collins

"Personal travel accounts seem to be out of vogue at the moment, at least that's how I see it, although you may find other publishers express different views." - Weidenfeld & Nicolson. I didn't.

"Your travels sound very interesting. Sadly though while travel books enjoyed a vogue in the 80s, they are having a tougher time in the 90s." - Phoenix.

"We have found that the market for travel literature has declined from its high point a few years ago, and I don't think your memoir, however sincere and well expressed could work for us at the moment." - Hutchinson.

"I am afraid that because of the current market recession...." - Little Brown

The publishers John Murray, known for travel books, had a very interesting approach. I heard them taking part in a Radio 4 interview with comments like "We are always interested in a good travel book," or something along those lines. The response to my approach: "We regret, John Murray have ceased to consider unsolicited typescripts or publishing proposals...We advise authors in the first instance to approach a literary agent..." You have to be fairly well known already to get an agent interested, so this was a non-starter for a newcomer.

And this one I just had to include because I will never know if it was true or the greatest way to get rid of someone: "My apologies for not returning this sooner. Mr...(the publisher) died in March."

Well that is a cheerful note if you are just about to contact a publisher with ideas of your great new travel book. I would point out, however, that you do need to be extremely thick-skinned and not take no for an answer. I suppose you do have to take death as a definite 'no', but don't let other rejections deter you from approaching someone else. They are just part of this business whether you are trying to sell a book or an article and should never be taken personally. In fact if you receive anything other than a standard rejection slip, such as a few helpful comments from the editor, it should be seen as very positive encouragement.

These rejections, as I mentioned before, were three years ago and things do indeed go in trends. The market today is completely different. I don't know quite how the publishers have managed it, given that it could easily take three years for a book to come to fruition from its original conceptual ideas, but the travel books are back on the shelves.

A resurgence in interest in travel stories is upon us. Nearly all the publishers are bringing out new travel series. If you want to sell your book to a publisher you must have some idea of what is selling at the moment. It could save you a great deal of time. The easiest way is to go into a bookshop and have a look. I did just that in my local branch of Waterstone's just to see what they are offering. It is a fair representation of what the publishers are publishing.

The classic travel writers are still being cajoled into finding new work. Look at the rows of books by Sir Wilfred Thesiger. He has just brought out a new one called 'The Danakil Diary' which is indeed a hitherto unpublished work. The travel to which it relates, however, is anything but new. He wrote the original diary in 1933-34 when he was just 23. Whilst he is unquestionably a genius of the travel writing genre, I have to wonder why he has chosen to publish this so long after the event. Although produced by a different publisher the new book sells alongside 'Arabian Sands', first published in 1959.

Look at the rows of books by Dervla Murphy all in matching covers like a matching new series. I picked one from the shelf at random. 'Full Tilt' was the title; it was published by Flamingo in 1995, but was first published by John Murray in 1965. Has travel really not changed in 30 years?

There are still books being published to coincide with TV programmes, like Great Railway Journeys with stories by TV personalities like Victoria Wood. And I noticed a book by Clive

Anderson in the travel section, which is again making the most of a known TV connection.

There are a whole host of books by people whom we all recognise as travel writers such as Paul Theroux, Colin Thurborn, Bill Bryson, Eric Newby and Nick Danziger to mention just a few. Some have been writing for decades and some for several years. One thing they all have in common is that at the present time they can be considered to be established writers. Nicholas Crane, whose latest book 'Clear Water Rising' has just been published, certainly had no trouble finding a publisher for his work. He gives us an insight into the experience in chapter 13.

It may come as a surprise, but they are not the only writers getting published. Several new books really caught my eye, not through familiarity but completely the opposite. There are new authors in the travel section for the first time in years. I suppose there will always be, and to an extent always has been, room in the market for people who have done something really out of the ordinary or who have a name that will stick in your mind. The book 'The girl who walked her dog 4,500 Miles' by Spud Talbot-Ponsonby perhaps fits this category.

What interested me more was that there are books by completely unknown everyday people who have gone out and done some travelling. Travel is always an adventure to those taking part and you don't actually have to be a great explorer or find some gimmick. If your travels were exciting, why shouldn't they make an interesting book, whatever the traditional publishing houses think?

Tony Wheeler who started the Lonely Planet Guides could well be on to a winner with his new series of travel literature. He has brought out a series called 'Journeys' which are quite simply travel books that people have written about their travel experiences.

Some of the books are indeed written by established writers like Isabella Tree, but others are written by newcomers to the genre. The journal styled 'Sean & David's Long Drive' is a case in point. If publishers are realising that ordinary journeys can make extraordinary reading, then we will see far more travel books by new writers.

I don't for a moment think it is easy to get a book into print, but I think there is a better chance now than there has been for many years.

When you are first setting your goals on a career in travel writing I'm not sure that travel literature is the way to make an easy start. However it is a very valid part of the market and some people do make a go of it.

Guide Books

I briefly touched on the subject of guidebooks in chapter 2 under the section on paid commissions. Most people who write a guide book are in fact being commissioned to do so. I can't really imagine writing a guide to a country and then trying to sell it to a publisher on spec. On the other hand that is how most of the guide book publishers started out, writing a single guide and publishing it themselves.

I don't think those same opportunities still exist today. When Tony Wheeler, the founder of Lonely Planet, started up, he wrote 'Across Asia on the Cheap' based on his own travel experience. At that time there simply weren't any other guides of the type. Lonely Planet has grown to become one of the largest travel publishers in the world and has guides to almost anywhere you can think of. Similarly Hilary Bradt of Bradt Guides started with her own experiences of trekking in Peru and Bolivia. There just weren't any other books on the subject at the time.

Although there are always new destinations and new angles you would have to be pretty lucky to be ahead of the major publishing houses and come up with something that you could start your own guide book company with. Even if you wanted to write about a new destination for one of the existing companies you would have to be quick off the mark.

In '94 I got a photographic commission to go to Eritrea and Ethiopia. At that time there weren't any guides and I thought I may just have hit on a new destination and could do some ground work on my first visit. I approached several publishers with differing responses.

Rough Guides loved the idea but felt that they had other priorities. They still have many more popular destinations in the pipeline for new guides and didn't want to invest in this particular destination. Lonely

Planet were really enthusiastic. They wrote back to me agreeing with me that it was a really good idea. In fact, it was such a good idea that "...unfortunately we have already commissioned such a book and a team of writers has commenced working on it...". Bradt Guides' "Guide to Eritrea" was the first and made it into print about a week before I flew out to Africa.

This little story may show that I was too late for the idea, but it also confirms the point that there are still new destinations and new guides being brought out. I may have missed the boat, but *somebody* had got the job.

Guide books are a huge section of the travel publishing industry. As well as new destinations, all the old guide books need regular updating if they are going to be of any use to travellers. All this is work for the travel writer and good experience for future projects. If this type of writing appeals to you, even if you don't want to do it full time, it is well worth looking into the opportunities this market offers.

I spoke to Pat Yale who is a regular writer for Lonely Planet to find out her views on guide book writing. I was rather pleased to find her very enthusiastic about the potential of this type of travel writing:

"Working for Lonely Planet you can make a living. I'm not in any doubt about that," she told me.

She did go on to qualify this statement though, saying that there was an enormous amount of work involved and if you were to work out all the hours you spent on the project, particularly taking into account the months spent away researching the area, the hourly rate wouldn't work out too well.

There is also the consideration that not all guide books work on the same payment scales. She had been approached by Blue Guides to do a book on Vietnam for a fixed fee. The amount of money offered was small to say the least and out of that fee all the travel expenses had to be paid. It was to be a cultural guide so there was a great deal of work to be done and it was to cover the entire country from scratch. She knew that there would be no archival documents in Vietnam itself so she would also need to go to France to check on colonial archives. How else can you get accurate information about the cultural monuments? While all this travelling might be great fun, at the end of the day, most people still have a mortgage to pay back home. From her point of view the project was a non-starter just because of the lack of adequate financial reward.

She felt that some guide book publishers based their offers on the assumption that a certain amount of facilities might be provided to you for free. There might well be airlines or hoteliers that are prepared to offer their services, but it seems a little unkind to expect the writer to have to sort this out or else be out of pocket.

My own experience of guide book publishers is somewhat similar. Mark Ellingham, the founder of Rough Guides, was very happy to consider me for updating work on his guides. He gave me a list of his update schedule for the next five years and said for me to let him know what area I would be interested in. "The only thing is," he added "we won't pay you." Of course my expenses would have been paid so I would at least have got free travel, but you have to think quite hard if free travel is a big enough reward.

I do think that when you are starting out there is a need for free travel and this sort of project could well fit in with other plans. After all you are not going to be writing the guide book day and night and can make the most of the trip by writing articles and taking photos at the same time. You can never afford to close any door and must explore every avenue that is open to you. Free travel is a start and the offer I got from Rough Guides was certainly the best offer I'd had all day. Perhaps one day I will take them up on it.

Pat Yale also warned of the problems associated with this line of work. Not least was the fact that you are away for so long that it is very difficult to do any other work. "That means that you have got all your eggs in one basket which is risky, and it makes it difficult to break out of it into something else."

This is, however, all a matter of how you approach the project. If you know that you are going to do the guide for the sake of the free travel then there is no reason why you shouldn't be able to write articles and take photographs at the same time, although the amount of time required to pursue this is something of a limiting factor. It takes so long to research the guide, and then the manuscript has to be completed when you get back from the destination. It's not impossible though. Pat herself has had articles published after having written her pieces for the Lonely Planet and also admits: "I'm not a very pushy person and I don't think I exploit fully the openings that are there. I'm pretty sure that someone else could take more advantage of the trips than I do.".

I went on to ask Pat about taking photographs and whether she sees this as being an integral part of the job. It turns out that it is not just advantageous, but a requirement of Lonely Planet for their writers to provide some photos that can be used in the book. At one time they didn't pay for these, but their new contracts actually give the author an extra payment if their photos are used.

This is what Pat had to say about her photography:

"I'm not a good photographer. I can take a perfectly decent snapshot which is useable for their (Lonely Planet's) purposes if they don't want anything particularly clever, but I know nothing about photography and I'm not a good photographer. I couldn't sell my slides to slide libraries; I'm sure they wouldn't be remotely good enough, but I think the opening is there."

Despite this view of her capabilities she went on to tell me that the publishers had used one of her photos for nothing less than the front cover of their guide to Ireland. I'm quite sure that they would not have used a photo just because it was free. Their cover is their image and if she can take photos good enough for a front cover she has what it takes to be a photographer.

Of course I accept that not everybody wants to expand the photography side of their work, but look at the potential if you do. If you have to take these travel photos anyway it seems a shame not be taking it seriously and just treating that part of the work as an aside.

There were a few other things that I learnt about guide book writing during my conversation. It is not just the publishers that commission people to write guide books. Very often the commissioned author will sub-contract. This is standard practice. An author who agrees to do an update, for example, will realise that he can not cover the whole of a country on his own. Rather than the publisher having to employ several authors they will leave it in the hands of one principle author who contracts out different sections of the book to different people. He then has to pay them out of his fee rather than the publisher paying them. This could mean that you have got just as much chance of getting work from a fellow writer as from a publisher.

It has to be said that sometimes this can get right out of hand. I'm told that some commissioned authors have been known to sub-contract to such an extent that all they are actually doing is taking the credit and a chunk of the money.

You might wonder at what stage you can actually get your hands on the money when you are undertaking such a large project as a guide book. Obviously with a fixed fee there is the risk that you blow it all while you're doing the research and you have nothing left by the time you get home. In general, if you are contracted to Lonely Planet, you get your money in three parts. A good half of the money is paid in advance, then the bulk of the remainder is paid six weeks after you deliver your manuscript and the balance is paid on publication. They are also very prompt payers so you don't have the hassle of chasing them up for your money.

Pat Yale's final tip on the subject was that there is a distinct lack of women writers in the guide book business. It could well be that the lifestyle of travelling alone is less appealing to women; in any case it seems that fewer women approach publishers. If they are actually trying to increase their list of female authors there could be excellent opportunities here for women writers.

A word of warning if you are considering any kind of contract: it is all very well taking a conscious decision to do something knowing that you are not going to get the credit, or in some cases any payment, but you have to be aware of just what the deal is. Whilst I do advocate doing something for nothing if you can see a long term reason for it, there are always those who would take advantage. It would be easy to be so keen to get into print that you sign away all your rights. Some people have even been asked to sign contracts guaranteeing that they will not write anything else about the destination for any other publication. This is not only a ridiculous suggestion to a travel writer, it may also preclude you from writing the article which is your only intended source of profitability from the whole deal. It is always worth getting in print to further your own credibility as a writer, but don't let anybody feather their nest at your expense. The idea is to make it pay for you, not for somebody else.

Photographs in this book

The photographs in this book have all been included to illustrate certain points. They may have helped me to make money by being sold, either along with an article or separately, or they may be to illustrate the use of certain photographic techniques or particular equipment. The first of the four colour sections starts on the opposite page, but when you want to know a little more about the pictures turn to chapter 11. There you will find a full explanation of the points I am making.

Pigs in Paradise, Honduras - page 162

*Tanks, Travellers and
Local Transport,   Eritrea*
- page 164,165

Pushkar Camel Fair, Rajasthan, India - page 166

Leaning Tower of Pisa, Italy
- page 166

Eiffel Tower at Night, Paris
- page 167

Spider Monkey, Costa Rica - page 162

Chapter 4

Markets for travel photography

The markets for photography are just as complex as the markets for writing that I considered in chapter 3. Similarly, many of these markets will require both words and pictures, but in this chapter I want to concentrate on the picture aspect of those markets.

Newspapers

The national papers use travel photographs to compliment the travel articles they publish. It is quite unusual for them to run a picture-led travel feature, but they do buy pictures and indeed do also use pictures that are not directly related to an article.

I always submit a picture or two with the article in the first instance - this takes the form of a laser print about which I go into greater detail in chapter 7. This ensures that the editor knows right from the beginning that if photos are required to accompany the piece, you have them available and are happy to supply them. Your own photos will be precisely relevant to an article that you have written and, if you are taking the photography seriously, they will be far more suitable than anything the paper might find elsewhere.

Depending on the paper in question, some of the articles that are published will be words only, and often just a couple of the articles have photos. It takes time and effort for a busy picture editor to find suitable photos and the simple fact that your piece comes as a potential package with excellent photos might mean that yours is the one they use as their illustrated piece.

Profitability is vastly increased at this point. You can expect to receive anything upwards from about £65 per photo. The actual fee paid depends on the paper you are dealing with and also on the size of the photo reproduction, but it is not uncommon to receive £100 or so. Colour reproduction usually commands a higher price. This isn't money for nothing, as there are considerable costs involved in producing these photos in the first place, but it certainly can increase revenue by a vast proportion.

Given that not everybody will supply photos with their written work, the newspapers do have to look for illustrations elsewhere. This is just as important a market for us but extremely difficult to break into. Most picture editors have a good working relationship with a number of slide libraries. They can contact a library, say what they want and have a mass of high quality material arrive on their desk. The chances are they will find something which will work with the story. I think it is fair to say that these editors do not have the time to deal with hundreds of individual photographers, each of whom have only limited stock.

If you are gradually building up your travel experience and your personal library of images, though, there should come a time when you have something to offer on a regular basis.

Once you feel you have something to contribute there is nothing to stop you from submitting photos to the picture editor just as the libraries do, in order to have your photos used with somebody else's piece. It doesn't happen very often, but it does happen. For example The Mail on Sunday used a photograph of mine to illustrate an article on Honduras that was written by one of their staff writers.

Photograph usage is not limited to article illustration. In the Saturday travel section of The Daily Telegraph there is a *'Where in the world?'* competition which is based on a photograph of a famous but slightly out of the ordinary scene. This type of specific requirement may be difficult to find in a slide library but you could have a selection of images that would be just the job. If you spot something like this, it is worth contacting the picture desk and finding out if they would like you to submit some of your work.

It is much easier to make an approach when you have a specific usage in mind. Lists of the stock you have available are all very well but I think they would probably get filed away and only looked at if all the normal sources had failed. By that time your lists would probably be out of date. If your initial approach with a picture for a specific usage is successful, it gives you a foot in the door for the future.

<u>Magazines</u>

Magazines differ from newspapers in some very important ways. They use photographs as far more of an integral part of their image. They do use pictures to accompany articles but many magazines also have picture-led features and virtually every mainstream consumer magazine has a cover photo. The quality of the reproduction of the photographs is completely different from newsprint and so your best images will look far better in a glossy magazine than reproduced in black and white on newspaper.

Most of the comments I have made about newspapers similarly apply to magazines so I won't say it all again, but there are added opportunities here.

You can approach magazine editors with ideas for photo-led features just as you would put in a proposal for an article. The photographs may be run as a photo essay or the magzine could even like the photos so much that they commission an article to compliment them. I was recently commissioned to write an article about the Upper Nile region of Egypt to complement photographs that a magazine had already agreed to use. OK, on this occasion I was doing the words not the photos, but I was interested to learn that a well-known photographer had managed to sell the photographs alone. It just shows the high profile and importance that is placed on photographs for magazines. If they are good they will sell on their own and the publication will go to considerable lengths to find the words to accompany them.

Front covers are also of huge importance. To an extent they sell the magazine and certainly represent the image of the product that the publishers want to portray. The cover photograph also commands the highest payment and certainly the greatest prestige. Payments are usually twice that of the rate paid for a full page inside the magazine itself.

Some magazines use a cover that relates to an article, hence a cover story, but others place more importance on an image for the magazine. They will use photographs that have no relevance to a particular article but that really say what they want to be said about the style of the magazine itself. These images can therefore be submitted well in advance regardless of the editorial features lists and indeed you should always think of the cover shot potential when you are out taking the photographs in the first place. Some magazines will actually commission the photographers in order to get the front covers that they want, but this is expensive and a suitable image sent in on-spec will be well received.

The process of taking a cover shot takes a bit of forethought. Think of the magazine that you are targeting and get to know their style. Whilst it is normal to try to take photos in which the image fills the frame, this is not ideal for a cover. A cover needs to be in portrait format (vertical) and it needs to have space for the printing to go over the top without spoiling it. This might mean a larger-than-normal margin of sky to allow for the magazine title, or non-critical space at one side of the subject to allow for the details of the magazine's contents to be printed.

Books

It is worth making yourself known to publishers of travel books, particularly the guide book companies. They are continually bringing out new titles and revising old titles. Every new edition has a new cover and that usually means new photos are needed.

Books are a very long time in the planning and guide book publishers may have a schedule of production that stretches many years ahead. If they have seen a photo that really catches their eye and would suit their cover, this could be decided long in advance. On the other hand finding just the right cover often proves a problem and if you can find out what is coming up in the future you can at least try to get the shots specifically for that book. The guide books (with the exception of the highly pictorial guides) try to get their cover shots from the author of the guide. If that fails they move on to enquire from known photographers, and only then do they put out their requests to libraries so there is a very good chance of sucess in dealing with these publishers direct.

The large publishing houses also have a huge appetite for good quality photographs. It may not immediately strike you that travel photographs have any place in anything other than travel books, but this would be taking far too narrow a point of view. Think of all the hundreds of reference and educational books that have illustrations. The sort of photographs that they use are images from around the world and that is potentially within our scope.

There are books on geology that need pictures of rock formations, geysers, deserts and volcanos. Geography books need images ranging from tropical vegetation to reservoirs and rainstorms. Anthropology reference books need pictures of tribal people from far flung locations or pictures that show the society of ancient civilisations; images of monuments, ruins, artworks, even skeletons and museum exhibits have their place in these pages. Some publishers use images that you wouldn't even associate with the topic of their book, but for one reason or another they fit the text or make a statement. For example one of my volcano shots, in the same series as the front cover of this book, has just been used by the publishers Hodder & Stoughton Educational in an English language teaching book.

I could go on, but I think you get the picture; and if you've got the picture - sell the picture!

Cards and posters

There are literally thousands of cards and posters produced each year and many of them will use a photographic image as their base. It is quite normal for these markets to want exclusivity and world rights over the pictures they buy. This is because the picture itself is their product rather than the picture being used to sell something else or to illustrate part of a larger work. Exclusivity means higher prices. Figures of £200 upwards for world postcard rights for a five year period are not uncommon. That is quite a reasonable fee for a single photograph and even if you have sold the postcard rights you can still sell the same image to magazines or any other market that is not in direct competition with the postcards. The fee for posters is sometimes calculated on a royalty basis depending on sales, rather than a flat fee.

This type of market, and I should perhaps include calendars in this section, is quite lucrative, but the buyers have very exacting requirements.

Travel companies

Tour operators and travel agents, airlines, ferries, land transport companies and hotels have all got brochures and promotional literature. How many travel brochures can you think of that don't have photographs? I can think of one which has excellent drawings as its illustrations, but that is about it - one.

Highly illustrated brochures can prove to be a very expensive thing to produce and a huge proportion of a company's marketing budget will go on this single item. It is their main sales tool and extremely important to them. In order to reduce production costs many companies will use photographs that have been taken by their staff and customers. That is all very well if they can get enough images of a high enough quality to promote their product.

Others will use slide libraries to a varying extent. They may produce a complete brochure from library shots, or they may get the bulk of their photographs from staff and the remainder from a library - especially the cover shot. This does keep their costs down and can work extremely well.

Slide libraries tend to be very expensive and you can often find companies that need a great deal of photos but just can't afford to buy them all from a library. They nevertheless want something of a professional standard.

If you have made yourself known to the staff that develop and produce the brochures, there is every chance that they will consider your relevant work in preference to a library. They seem to like dealing with photographers because if you have taken a photo yourself you will know exactly where and when it was taken and if it will fit the use that it is required for. Picture researchers in a library have a tremendous knowledge and will have captions and cross-references to help them identify an image, but it is not the same as actually talking to the photographer. If a tour operator is trying to sell a specific trip it isn't good enough to have a photograph that is almost the right place - it has to be precise or they could end up in all sorts of tricky situations.

They can also usually negotiate a mutually beneficial price from a photographer that they might not be able to get from the library. It is dangerous to undercut a library and end up spiking the system and devaluing the work, but there are occasions when low prices can work for you. Certain travel companies are so low budget that they will simply not use the photos if they can't get them at the right price. You are not doing a library out of business, because the alternative would be for them to use their own photos. It is better to get some money and get some photos published than to get nothing and have them use neither your work nor a library's.

So direct sales of individual photographs or packages of photographs is a strong possibility in this sphere.

Several travel companies have a greater photographic requirement than for the brochure alone. They give promotional slide shows which cover all aspects of their trips. In order to have the right shots at hand whenever they want them for brochures, adverts, promotions and slide shows, they build up their own libraries of photographic images. Of course there will be staff and customers that offer their pictures for low prices or even free just to see their pictures in print, but if they use a lot of photos this just won't be sufficient.

Their best bet is to commission a photographer to provide them with a library of images that they can use as and when they want to. This is a very good opportunity for any travel photographer. I touched on the subject in chapter 2 under the heading of paid commissions, but I will give a little more detail here.

In these situations you have to work out what the travel company wants and how badly they want it. You can start with the premise that they want the photographs and you want to go and take them, but there is still a whole range of financial circumstances that might apply, as I am about to explain. The chances are that you will be approaching them rather than them approaching you.

If they have lots of photos, but could always do with some new ones, then they will not be too bothered whether you go or not. A free trip might cost the company next to nothing if it is just one place within a group of paying customers. They might therefore be very happy to give you a free trip. If they *need* the photos then they will be prepared to up the stakes, starting with including the cost of your flights, increasing to include expenses and culminating in paying you a fee. This top end of the scale will also vary from a token gesture to a full blown photographic fee based on your day rate charges. Generally the longer the commission the less you will get paid on a per day basis.

The rights that you sell for these photos will also make a difference to the cost. If you are going to be able to go somewhere you really want to get to and think you will be able to take lots of images that you can sell elsewhere then obviously it makes sense to consider a commission even if it is just for a free trip - especially when you are just starting up and you are trying to build up your own experience and your own photo library.

As a travel writer and photographer you have an advantage over people that are just travel photographers in this particular section of the market. You will of course end up writing about the trip that you make - the travel experience whilst out on the photographic commission. As travel companies are always trying to get themselves written about this could be an opportunity for them. You can't promise anything if you don't genuinely have a commission for an article in advance, but you can certainly make your intentions known and this could well put you ahead of the competition. You also have to bear in mind that the company might not be particularly good and not one that you would want to mention in an article anyway. Never commit yourself to being nice about something before you know you can be.

If all goes well you should be able to take the photos to fulfil the commission, take photos that you can sell to other markets and write articles about your travels - which you will sell illustrated with your own photographs of course.

All you need to know about copyright of photographs

The very first principle is that a photographer automatically has copyright over his own photographs. No one can initially use the photographs without obtaining permission from the photographer.

How the photographer passes on these rights is all important. Rights are usually sold specific to usage, passing on only those rights that the buyer actually needs. This leaves you free to sell other rights to other customers.

Restrictions can be placed on the geographical area in which those rights have been sold and a certain time limit can be placed on those rights.

Selling a photograph with an article into a British publication you would sell Single British Rights. That would mean that the publication had the right to use the photograph once, in Britain only. This is a non-exclusive arrangement. That is to say several publications could have these rights at the same time, allowing you to sell the picture again and again.

You do not have to specify a geographical area. A publication may be distributed in several countries or even published in more than one country. If you sell Single Reproduction Rights and specify that it is for use in a particular publication then there can be no misunderstandings over what has been sold.

Buyers might specify that they want an amount of exclusivity, and for this they would normally pay higher prices. For example they might buy the rights for a period of five years and exclude you from selling the image to any directly competing market. This would be quite normal for a greetings card or postcard rights.

A travel company might specify that the photo they buy for their brochure must not be sold to any competing travel company brochures for a period of a year while their brochure is in circulation.

Anyone who has commissioned a photograph for advertising purposes will probably want to buy the copyright outright. Commissioning firms may think that they have rights to everything you take whilst on the commission and if this is not your intention it is very important to make this clear.

Don't give away rights that the customer doesn't need because once they have those rights you relinquish your interests.

Beware of competitions - some entry rules give the organisers all rights to the pictures submitted whether they are winners or not. It would be a pretty low act, but technically a good picture could end up being used for very valuable advertising without payment to the photographer.

When you lodge work at a picture library you are agreeing that the library have the authority to sell rights on your behalf. They will not sell anything outright without your permission and you also have to agree not to sell the rights elsewhere in any way that might conflict with their marketing initiatives.

Travel products

Just as the tour operators need photographs of their trips and destinations, retailers and producers of travel-related products need photos of their merchandise on location. There are all kinds of these products, such as tents and sleeping bags, clothing for travellers and health products. Companies want shots of things like a particular mosquito net being used in a jungle somewhere, or a brand of walking boots shot at the top of Mt Kilimanjaro. I'm not suggesting that you do entire catalogue shoots, but there are always those one-off opportunities. Somebody always wants a photograph of their product in an unusual place.

For example there is a classic shot, that is frequently used in advertisements, of a Maasai warrior looking through a state of the art camera. I don't know the history of that particular shot but there is every chance of taking something like that on spec if you're always thinking of the potential rather than waiting to be commissioned.

Some companies are prepared to sponsor unusual travel plans just to promote their name and often require photographs of their products in action to support their investment in this sponsorship. It is worth considering if it will help you pay for your travels, but it is quite hard to get a sponsorship deal and they will want something in return. It could end up being more trouble than it is worth, making yourself beholden to somebody else's commercial requirements.

Slide libraries

However good you are at marketing, selling and getting yourself known, you will never be able to replace the services of a good slide library, at least not if you are going to be a travel writer and photographer. There is only so much time in a year and if your intentions are to spend a part of the year travelling, writing and taking photographs, you need help when it comes to selling your work.

A slide library is, to all intents and purposes, acting as a partner with you in your photographic work. You take the photos, they sell them and you split the money fifty fifty. It sounds great, but unfortunately that is over-simplifying the situation somewhat.

A slide library is looking for extremely high quality images from a photographer that is going to continue to travel on a regular basis. It is of absolutely no interest to them to have 20 great photos from your last holiday and never get another submission from you. The principles of quantity have a huge bearing on this industry.

A slide library has literally thousands, if not tens of thousands of photographic images on file. The libraries that are successful are the ones that can always find a photograph to match their customers' requests. They often specialise within a certain area, such as the general topic of travel, but within that topic the more diverse the images that they keep in stock, the greater the chances of meeting the requirements of the customer. They need to constantly update their image stocks and to expand them to cover new areas, different angles of the same area and even the same photographic subject under different lighting conditions or in different weather and seasons.

Working with several photographers the library is able to build and maintain this sort of collection. You need to be able to offer them hundreds of photographs and to keep offering them more stock to build up the amount of your work that they are offering out. They might well be selling hundreds of photographs every day, but very few of them will be yours if you only have a few lodged in a huge library.

A library will have contacts with hundreds of markets that you just don't have time to investigate or pursue. I mentioned having had a photo published in an educational book that had nothing to do with travel. This was a library sale as there is absolutely no way I would even have thought of contacting Hodder and Stoughton Educational to tell them I've got some great travel pictures. They, on the other hand, have a working relationship with slide libraries and contact the libraries for their picture requirements. This is a sale I would not have made without the library.

Not only do the libraries want quality and quantity, they also want a certain amount of commitment. Many of the agreements that are offered by libraries insist on exclusivity. You are asked to sign away your rights to market the photographs elsewhere for a given period of years while the photographs are at the library.

It is based on sound principles. The library doesn't want to be in a position where it is offering out your images to customers only to find that the customers are being offered those very same images, or ones just like them, from another library or from the photographer himself. You could end up in competition with yourself.

On the other hand, if you are intending to make the most of your photos, you want to be able to sell directly to the contacts you have made and to sell your images with your articles. It takes a certain amount of mutual understanding to find a library that are happy to work with you on this basis. You also have no guarantee that the library will actually sell anything on your behalf. Imagine the frustration if you sign all the photos over to someone who had exclusivity on them for five years and then they don't sell anything. You may know full well that you could have sold at least some of them but are restricted by the contract you have signed. It's quite a tough decision to make.

There are travel photographers who put all their faith into a particular library and derive all their income from that. It is certainly possible for the very best photographers and it must be quite good not to have to deal with the marketing side of your business.

There are always ways to work around or in sympathy with exclusivity clauses but you have to make sure all concerned are happy with the arrangements. If you know you are going to write an article you can easily withhold the particular photos that you want and not submit them to the library until after they have been published - this keeps everyone happy. It is often a very different sort of photographic subject that makes a good stock photograph than the sort of subject you want for your articles. An article photo needs to be very specific to illustrate your words, but a good library shot is one that can be used again and again in all sorts of different applications.

I think the slide library has a very important place as part of a balanced marketing strategy for your work. I wouldn't want to rely on it to make my living out of this and nothing else, but there is something rather good about getting a cheque in the post at the end of each quarter and finding out that your work has been published in places you have never even thought of.

Markets for travel photography

It is not my intention to make this chapter a definitive reference on all the markets for travel photography and you should certainly look at the many market reference books that are available. What I have tried to do, however, is to state the need to be aware of the market potential for travel photography. There is so much more to it than just taking a few snaps to go with your articles and, for me anyway, it has been a very valuable part of the business. The essential thing is to take it seriously and to have markets in mind when the camera is in your hand. If you are looking out for images when you're travelling there is every chance of seeing something and thinking 'that would make a great greetings card, a stock shot, or a front cover for such-and-such magazine', rather than just thinking 'I'll get a shot of this landscape so that my article can show where I've been'.

Market reference books

I mentioned in the previous chapter that there are listings of magazines, newspapers and book publishers in both *The Writer's Handbook* (Macmillan) and the *Writers' & Artists' Yearbook* (A&C Black). Both books actually give far more information than that, such as lists of broadcasting companies, literary agents, picture libraries, societies and organisations and so on.

The Freelance Photographer's Market Handbook is produced annually by the Bureau of Freelance Photographers and is directed specifically at the photographer. This gives similar listings, but includes the name of the relevant picture editor who is often not the same person as the overall editor. It also lists agencies, libraries, card and calendar publishers, and useful services to photographers amongst its contents.

Chapter 5

Tools of the trade

There are a whole range of useful tools available to the serious travel writer and photographer. The tools you actually need are not quite the same as what you might like to have, and certainly a whole lot different from how much you can afford.

I never like to buy anything without justifying the expense and if you are going into this as a business that is a fairly sound practice. I am sure some people will want to treat travel writing and photography as a hobby and I can not begin to say what tools they would want to acquired under those circumstances. What someone can afford to spend on a hobby is what they are prepared to spend on their entertainment.

Having said that I would regard some things as essentials and others as luxuries. For anyone hoping to profit from their endeavours it is essential to make an investment in what can be considered tools of the trade. I would strongly recommend you not to go over the top though, as expensive equipment will not sell the end product.

I started out with old, secondhand, borrowed and very cheap equipment. As my work has progressed I have added to it, replaced it and bought new state-of-the-art kit. The level at which you start off must depend on how much you can afford to invest, and whether or not you can really expect profits to justify the investment. Expectations, hopes and budgets always turn out to be very different from actual income and profit.

Tools for writing

Word processors

This I would consider to be an absolute, top-of-the-list essential. Anyone who is serious about writing will find a way to get access to a word processor. The modern technological society has moved on a little from hand-written manuscripts which are then typed, although I am constantly surprised at the number of advertisements offering typing services to writers. In this day and age almost everyone has access to a word processor. Even the kids at primary schools have computers. I do, of course, realise that not everybody has used one and may not know their way about the different functions and programmes that are available.

Hardware

Writing doesn't require a great deal of computer power or memory. The simplest of machines will handle an amount of word processing. This is good news if you are just starting up because it means that yesterday's technology is adequate for the writer's needs. I started out borrowing an old Amstrad from a friend. It was not powerful enough for his business, but easily ran a word processing package.

Even if you can't borrow one there are cheap and secondhand machines on the market that will do the job. It is very tempting to want the best, top-of-the-range computer but even that will be out of date within a year, so you might as well save money and buy one that is already out of date. Start-up costs need to be kept down.

Because the computer industry does move so quickly there is little point in making recommendations as to the particular specifications you need from your hardware. I think the rule of thumb will always be to choose 'the most recent of yesterday's technology at an affordable price'.

Software

Word processing packages are many and varied. There is no need to get anything very complicated or powerful for simple pages of text. The newer versions of the old programmes are certainly improved and easier to use. They are more versatile, performing more complex functions. For writing a page of text, however, all these clever functions are not needed. After all we are just using the machine as a glorified type-writer. The more complex the software, the bigger and more expensive the hardware you need to run it. What you can actually run will therefore depend on how down market you go with the hardware. You may find that you have to buy new software even if you acquire a secondhand machine - see warning below.

A few of the more common word processing programmes are Windows Write, Microsoft Word, Lotus Ami Pro and WordPro, WordPerfect and WordStar. Windows Write comes free with Windows but is really word processing at its simplest. The others all have a range of more complex functions.

Desk top publishing (DTP) packages can perform a much wider range of tasks. With these you can design and create the layout of pages, including placing graphics, pictures and text onto the page and have it put in all the printer's marks. A word processor is probably all you need to start with unless you are thinking of self-publishing your work.

There are a few computer functions that are invaluable to the writer and whatever package you decide to buy you should make sure that it has what you need. The most important functions are listed below.

Word Count

When you start writing you will find that the size of a piece of work is expressed by the number of words. In fact articles are sold by the number of words. Writing to a particular required length is absolutely essential. I have spent hours counting words as the programme that I started with didn't have a word count function. This is so frustrating and time consuming. A word count is an essential requirement.

Spelling

Most programmes have a function to check spelling. I find this useful but not everybody would. One of the drawbacks is that it gives a false sense of security. You can run the spell check and still have incorrect words in the text, e.g. if you have typed *of* when you meant to type *if,* the spell check does not recognise a mistake has been made.

Thesaurus and Grammar

Thesaurus and grammar checks are available, but I don't rate them very highly. This could just be due to my lack of experience in using them on the screen. You certainly do need a thesaurus and indeed a method of checking grammar usage if you are going to write for a living. I prefer to have these in book form rather than as a function of the word processor.

Other functions allow text to be copied, moved, deleted and generally played around with. The size, fonts and spacing of lines and words can be changed. These functions are common to all word processors but are more easily performed on some than others.

A word of warning - software programmes are subject to licensing agreements. If you buy a new machine (even if it is old technology) the agreements come with the package. This even applies to pre-loaded software. If you are buying a second-hand machine you may have no rights to use the software that is on it. You could be inadvertently breaking some licensing agreement between the software company and the original purchaser.

Printers

Writing on a word processor is all very well, but at some stage the writing has to be printed onto paper.

Dot matrix printers

The cheapest printers are dot matrix printers. These print out a series of dots which form the typed letters. The quality can be a little variable as the inked ribbons get fainter with use, just like a typewriter's. You can make do with this type of printer if you're on a very tight budget, but I don't think it will be long before you wish you had something better. I suspect dot matrix printers will soon be a thing of the past. The old ones have no resale value and I have just had to take mine down to the dump as there doesn't even seem to be a way to recycle them.

Ink jet printers

Ink jet printers are the next stage up. They have cartridges of ink that electronically squirt ink onto the paper. It is very precise and gives excellent quality. The black and white printers are within most budgets, and there is really no need to get a colour printer if you are only using it for text. The small extra cost over the dot matrix printers is easily worth it for the extra quality.

Laser printers

Laser printers start to get expensive. These produce an image in the same way as a photocopier does. The paper becomes electronically charged by an extremely accurate laser which writes its charged text in the precise shape of the typed letters. The ink then sticks to the charged area of the paper. This is the most accurate printer and produces the highest quality. For most of us, however, there is almost no way to justify the cost. There is really nothing wrong with the results from the cheaper printers.

Laptops

A laptop or portable computer is something that might be considered. I have found that it is extremely difficult to retain a disciplined writing routine whilst on the move. As travel is a major part of my life, I need to be able to write on the move.

I have become so accustomed to writing with a word processor that it is actually quite difficult to write anything but notes without one. A pencil and paper is all very well but there is a tendency to make notes all too brief. I always think I'll remember something if it is important but it is often the unimportant things, the asides, that really make a piece of writing interesting.

There is no substitute for immediacy and it is certainly helpful to be able to produce finished work while the subject is still very fresh in the mind.

Some of the trips I've done have taken me a couple of months. I cannot afford to be unproductive for such a long period. It means that so much work has to be done on my return that the whole trip never actually makes a profit. Whilst there is no travel writing without travel, the writing part of it must not go on hold for long periods of time.

A laptop is an expensive piece of equipment but if travel writing is your career it eventually becomes a justifiable expense. If you are going to want one in the long term it might be worth looking at them right from the start. Portable computers today are so sophisticated that there may be no need to have a desk-top computer as well.

The main drawback to having a laptop as your only computer is that the keyboards and screens are small. As a main office PC this could become quite frustrating. On the other hand most of the portables have all the right sockets to allow a separate screen and keyboard to be plugged into them. Some of them even have docking stations which expand the versatility of the machine. The docking station stays at home in the office whilst the smaller processing unit with screen and inbuilt keyboard can be detached and taken with you on your travels.

Deciding which laptop to buy

All the same principles of processing and memory capacity that I mentioned about computers in the hardware section, apply equally well to the laptops as to the desktops. Again it all depends on what programmes you want to run. Models with black and white screens are considerably cheaper although they seem to be going out of fashion. Most of the manufacturers are dropping the black and white models from their lists. This could be good news if the same principle of yesterday's technology being cheaper applies. There don't, however, seem to be many secondhand laptops on the market. As the stocks of the old black and white models run out it could just mean that there is no choice but to buy the more expensive colour models.

Power sources for laptops

The most important thing is to establish how you are going to power the unit whilst on the move. You need a battery facility and indeed need to carry a spare battery, as the charge does not last for long. Figures given for how long the battery lasts are a bit like fuel consumption figures for cars. They don't actually lie about them but they are based on factory tests that maximise the results. The actual field use figures will usually be considerably less. The extra batteries are very expensive.

You may also need a charger for the batteries and a mains adaptor. Some models have internal battery chargers and transformers so that they only need a mains lead. The current is transformed to the appropriate form and the batteries are charged just by plugging into the mains.

Car adaptors are also available so that the machine can be run from the cigarette lighter socket on a vehicle. There is a danger with the cheaper adaptors that they will not cope with any power surges. These are not uncommon in vehicles and the computer could be unprotected. The results could be as serious as a blown screen or losing all the stored memory. You need to consult the manufacturer to find out which car adaptors they will recommend. If you use one that they do not recommend you might find that the warranty does not cover any damage that occurs. This adaptor is another large expense, but without it the whole concept of portability is limited.

Tools for photography

35mm SLR cameras

The most basic essential tool for photography is the 35mm SLR camera. It is true that larger format cameras give a higher quality image but most people will find that carrying the necessary equipment for this is simply not practical if you're on the move. I would suggest that for the travel writer and photographer 35mm is the standard.

The SLR (single lens reflex) camera is what you might call a normal 'proper' camera. The image seen through the viewfinder is the actual image that comes through the lens and is reflected by a mirror up to the viewfinder - hence its name. Cameras which are not SLR rely on a viewfinder lens which is separate from the lens through which the image is photographed. They can be accurately used with experience but are largely responsible for all those holiday snaps that have people's legs or heads cut off. They obviously didn't look cut off through the viewfinder, but what could be seen through the viewfinder was not the same as the image the lens was actually going to receive.

The 35mm SLR is made up of a body and a detachable lens. A choice of different lenses can be fitted to the body. All the working parts of the camera have to put up with quite a lot of punishment if they are going to be used by a traveller. I have seen no end of cameras fall to pieces or stop working whilst on trips and there is usually no chance of getting them mended. It either happens in the middle of nowhere or just as you are about to leave the one place where you might have found a repair shop. If you are relying on these photos for your living and have commitments to fulfil then you have to get the photos, and a broken camera will just not do. It is therefore essential to have a robust outfit, a spare camera or both.

Camera bodies

There are two main classes of camera body that meet the requirement of being robust.

The first is the manual camera. These are simple with very few components that can go wrong. Many of the old ones have strong heavy bodies that will put up with an extraordinary amount of abuse. They will survive being dropped, will put up with extremes of climate and, because most of their workings are mechanical rather than electrical, they can even be used when the batteries have run out if necessary.

There are plenty of these on the secondhand market and they are cheap. Even the new ones are relatively inexpensive. The added bonus with this type of equipment is that even if it gets lost, stolen or damaged there is not a great deal of expense involved in replacing it.

Most of the major camera manufacturers have one of these simple cameras in their range or at least did have at some stage so you can still get them secondhand.

I am a big fan of the Pentax cameras. I have an old model called the ME Super which I bought thirteen years ago and it is still going strong. It has travelled all over the world with me and has been subject to all kinds of harsh treatment. I have used it to very good ends in deserts and rainforests, in extreme heat and cold and have even used it on high altitude treks. This camera has a choice of modes which include manual and some quite crude automatic modes (by today's standards).

I remember at one stage the back kept falling open and spoiling the films but in the absence of a repair man, I prized the back cover off its mountings and had a good look at it. It had become slightly bent but as it was made of a quite flexible metal, I was able to bend it back into shape. It has served me well ever since and still accompanies me on my travels, although in the past year it has been relegated to the spare camera status. I'm sure I could replace this camera body for less than a hundred pounds.

The other Pentax favourite is the K1000. This camera really has been around for years. It is completely manual without any automatic functions. A little needle in the viewfinder seems to be the only thing that the battery operates. This metering needle lets you know if you need to adjust the settings for the amount of light available. This camera has been so successful that Pentax actually relaunched it a few years ago. This means you don't have to get a second hand one if you don't want to, but can buy a brand new one for about £220. They really are so robust, however, that I can't imagine why you wouldn't buy a secondhand one.

The alternative class of robust camera bodies, I am sorry to say, is at the other end of the price scale. The higher your budget, the greater the choice of cameras that will come within your range.

Many of the mid-priced cameras are aimed at the amateur market. There is a tendency to include as many features as possible with any number of automatic modes. If you can understand how these modes work, which ones to use when and why, then you probably don't need them to be 'automatic'. Sometimes computing the mode can be more complicated than the principles of photography itself. These cameras appeal to people who think that the more buttons something has, the better it must be. I think that if you don't want to invest in the really good cameras, you might as well stay at the bottom end of the price range as delve into a market where manufacturers compete on gimmicks and jargon, rather than on performance and reliability.

Having said that, the cameras at the top-of-the-range of virtually all the manufacturers are absolutely superb. You can only compare like with like and I don't really want to get into a battle with camera manufacturers - I'll leave that to the numerous photo magazines that make their living from comparing similarly priced equipment. What I will do, though, is describe what I use and explain how I came to make this choice.

The Nikon F4S is the camera I use since I retired my old Pentax. Nikon have an excellent reputation for reliability and quality and it seems that lots of professionals use this top-of-the-range kit. The F4S is a derivative of the F4 and as far as I can make out is the most robust camera on the market. The new Nikon F5 is actually their top range model, but that has only just come out and wasn't on the market when I bought the F4. I'm sure the new model has lots of improvements and added features, certainly I have only heard good reports of it, but I don't think the F5 is within a beginner's price range anyway, being even more expensive than the F4.

The body is constructed from di-cast anti-corrosive aluminium alloy, giving it the strength that is so important although by necessity this means more weight. Everything that opens or shuts or moves is sealed with an O-ring. This keeps dust and moisture out of the internal workings.

The camera has a focusing system that allows for manual, autofocus or continuous autofocus. Autofocusing is a brilliant invention. It is fast and accurate, and has dramatically reduced the number of wasted shots that I get. It is still important to be able to manually focus because the camera doesn't know what the picture is that you are trying to take. It makes assumptions and can be fooled.

The internal metering system has a number of choices. It can take a reading from a single spot (spot metering), can give priority to the centre of the image for when the middle of the frame is the important thing (centre weighted), and can use its computerised system for looking at the overall image (matrix metering). This is done in a system of five sections which are analysed to compare brightness with contrast. This is known as a 5 segment matrix meter and the resulting computations give extremely accurate exposures. When you have a light meter that is this versatile built in to the camera there is no need to carry a separate hand held light meter.

The exposure settings can be left to automation or operated manually, with a good simple range of priorities.

There are several very clever features that I don't want to bore you with and, as I mentioned earlier, there are many comparisons that can be made with the top of the range models from other manufacturers.

The technical details are actually less important to me than the physical features. This camera feels good to hold and, even though it is quite big and weighty, it is easy to operate. There are no tiny switches or buttons that have to be pressed a certain number of times to get the required settings. Everything works on dials, catches and buttons that you can physically get hold of. It does seem to have been designed specifically to put up with hard use and to cope with hostile environments. As a travel photographer these are the considerations that far outweigh whether or not a camera has the very latest technical specifications. The Nikon F4S will score highly whatever your requirements are for a camera, but that is probably why it carries a price tag of almost two thousand pounds - and that's without a lens!

All you need to know about prime and marque lenses

A prime lens is one of a fixed specific focal length. They are the highest optical quality lenses. If you want to use prime lenses and have the scope to cover subjects with different focal length requirements, you need a range of different lenses.

Marque lenses are those lenses manufactured by the camera manufacturer, such as a lens made by Nikon for a Nikon camera, or Canon for a Canon camera etc.

Non-marque manufacturers such as Sigma, Tamron, Tokina and Vivitar specialise in lenses with a range of fittings. You choose the lens you want with the appropriate fitting for the camera you use. Tamron work on a system of detachable mounts so that you can use the same lens on cameras with different fittings. Each mount is effectively a marque-specific adapter.

Lenses

Although I have suggested using old and second-hand camera bodies when starting up, I would not apply the same arguments to the use of old lenses. There have been dramatic improvements in lens technology over the past years and even low budget new lenses will adequately complement the camera body you choose.

It is worth thinking about the medium and long term requirements at an early stage. If you are hoping to do this as a career and expect to upgrade your equipment in a few years' time then perhaps this should be reflected in your starting equipment. Compatibility of lenses to bodies is all-important. I took the view that I wanted the latest in lenses while I was still using my Pentax bodies. I had two Pentax bodies so the lenses were interchangeable. When I upgraded to the Nikon F4, however, all those lovely new lenses became surplus to requirements and I had to start all over again. They still serve a purpose as a complete spare kit, but this is not a cost-effective way of going about things.

Perhaps I should have stayed with Pentax cameras so that the lenses were still useful or maybe I should have bought an old Nikon in the first place, if I had thought that one day I might be able to upgrade to the F4. However things just didn't work out that way through lack of planning and foresight. I not only wanted to change to the Nikon but I wanted to get autofocus lenses at the same time. If I had initially started with an old manual Nikon I would still have been slightly caught out. I don't think I would have gone to the expense of getting autofocus lenses if I was unable to use the autofocus function; but in retrospect it would have been the sensible thing to do. Having said that, even the manual focus Nikon lenses would have been useful as Nikon have used the same fitting since 1959 so even old, as well as new, manual lenses would still have been compatible with my modern F4.

If you are just about to start out and need to buy some camera gear, perhaps you can benefit from my 20:20 hindsight vision, and think things out in advance.

When it comes to the actual specifications of the lenses you need, it is almost impossible to know where to begin and, more to the point, where to stop. As a travel photographer the range of subjects that you could potentially want to capture on film is very broad. Sometimes I find I am taking panoramic scenery shots and a moment later I might be taking close-up details of intricate designs, portraits of individual people or zooming in on some distant wildlife. It would be nice to have a different prime lens for each occasion but that just isn't practical. As a traveller everything I have has to be portable and versatile. One lens has to do more than one job.

All you need to know about f-stops

An f-stop or f-number is a unit of relative aperture. It is defined as the ratio of the lens focal length to the diameter of the entrance pupil. Confused? - So am I!

All you need to know is that it is the term used for the scale of aperture settings. Each step in the scale to the next f-number doubles (or halves) the exposure. All lenses focused to infinity transmit the same amount of light at a given f-number.
The scale's numerical series is:
f/1, f/1.4, f/2, f/2.8, f/4, f/5.6, f/8, f/11, f/16, f/22, f/32
Just to leave enough room for more confusion, the smallest f-number is the biggest aperture and the bigger the number the smaller the aperture.

Standard lenses

You might think that a 'standard lens' is the lens that comes with a camera when you buy it, i.e. it comes as standard. There is actually a technical meaning to the word standard, and such a lens may or may not be included with a camera body. The description is an expression of the focal length of the lens and is derived from the format of the film. It is equivalent to the diagonal length of a single frame of film. For 35mm films and cameras, which is the format I am confining my comments to, this measurement is about 50mm. So a lens with 50mm focal length is standard for our cameras. Anything less than 50mm is a wide-angle lens, and anything above 50mm is a telephoto.

A standard lens is a very good general purpose lens but lacks versatility as it just has the single focal length.

All you need to know about angle of view

If you hold your hands either side of your head and move them gradually out of your field of vision you will discover that our angle of view is almost 180°. At the extremes, though, you can hardly say that your hands are in clear view. You are aware of them out of the corners of your eyes, but they are blurred and distorted if you focus on an object immediately in front of you. The clear view in the centre of our vision only covers an angle of about 45°.

A 50mm standard lens has a field of view of 43° so it is very close to our own normal perception.

Wide angle lenses see more than our natural view and can therefore fit a large scene into a picture. Just like our eyes, these lenses can lose clarity and can distort the image at the extremities of the picture.

An ultra wide-angle lens of a focal length of about 16mm has an angle of view of about 180°. The picture produced includes considerably more than our own eyes can see clearly. These lenses are prone to distortion at the edges.

Telephoto lenses of greater than 50mm all concentrate on a small area. A 200mm lens, for example, only has a 12° angle of view.

Wide-angle lenses

These are lenses which have a wide angle of view. They give a greater depth of field than a standard lens or indeed the human eye. This exaggerates perspective. It can be used to good effect if you want the foreground to look larger than life but still have the distant objects in focus.

The lenses that are of most use are the 28mm and the 35mm. The single focal length lenses do tend to be very good quality, so it is worth getting one of these prime lenses if you are going to use it a great deal. You will definitely want some wide angle capability but might want to consider a zoom that includes these ranges, as it will be more versatile than the single focal length.

Ultra wide-angle lenses

These are lenses that have an even greater angle of view than the wide-angle. Anything less than about a 24mm could be considered an ultra wide-angle. The effects are further exaggeration of those I have mentioned for wide-angles. The nature of these lenses is such that the picture tends to distort at the edges but this can give an interesting image. Lenses at the widest end of the scale are special effects lenses known as 'fish-eye lenses'. These can be as wide as 8mm, giving a circular picture, or, at around 14-16mm, they fill the frame but still give considerable distortion. Trees in an avenue appear to curve over the top of the frame almost touching each other and forming a tunnel. These are great fun to play with and you can get saleable pictures from them, but they are certainly not on the list of essentials.

Lenses of less than about 20mm generally become very expensive although there are a few exceptions.

Vivitar make a 19mm lens that is very reasonably priced at around £100. Image quality is not always the best but it is still possible to get some spectacular results. By comparison Nikon have a 20mm priced at £620 or an 18mm at £1500!

Telephoto lenses

These are lenses that have a narrow angle of view. Their depth of field is narrow and they make distant objects appear to be close.

They aren't just for photographing things in the distance. Because of their ability to throw the background out of focus they are ideal for portraits. They can also be used to pick out and effectively highlight a subject from its surroundings.

Tools of the trade

How far do you want to see? If you are specialising in sport or wildlife you often need to be able to take subjects from a great distance. For all-round travel photography, though, this is not so important.

I would suggest you would want to go up to about a 200mm or at most a 300mm. The usual points apply to these prime lenses when compared with zoom lenses. The specific single focal length is limiting although of better quality. These are expensive lenses and unlikely to be versatile enough for the traveller. These prime lenses do, however, offer better optical quality and are often much faster lenses so you may want to consider one as part of a more comprehensive kit. The most useful is probably one at around 135mm. Nikon have one that is 135mm with an aperture of f2 at about £1300, or there are cheaper options from the non-marque brands.

This again is a non-essential, and I would steer you towards a zoom lens that covers the range.

All you need to know about lens speeds

Lenses are often referred to as being slow lenses or fast lenses. This is simply a function of the maximum aperture. A small aperture lets in less light than a large aperture. If less light is getting through this hole then it has to stay open longer for the emulsion on the film to react to it. A lens with a small maximum aperture is therefore slower than a lens with a large maximum aperture.

If you are taking action shots that require very fast shutter speeds, or want to take pictures in low light levels without using fast reacting films, you need a fast lens.

The fast lenses are more expensive. For example a Nikon zoom lens of 80-200mm with a maximum aperture of f4.5 costs about £250, but with a maximum aperture of f2.8 it costs about £1050.

Macro lenses

These are lenses that have the ability to focus on very close objects. They are capable of producing an image size that is from ½ life size up to a magnification of about 10 times life size. They have a very narrow depth of field which can make accurate focusing critical. These are specialist lenses and not an essential for the travel photographer. They

81

are, however, very useful if you want to take close up shots of flowers, insects or some other very small object that is typical of the place where you are travelling. So if you have got room and money it does add a valuable potential to your photography.

Many zoom lenses have a section at one end of their range which is marked as Macro but this is a poor substitute for a genuine specialist macro lens.

If you want to consider a macro, at the less expensive end of the market I would recommend the Tamron SP90mm f2.5. This lens will focus as close as 15 inches away. Its magnification allows ½ life-size images or, with the use of a special extension tube, up to life size images. It costs around £300. I get good results from it but I don't find that it gets an awful lot of use in the travel photography environment. Perhaps I should make the effort to use it more.

All you need to know about depth of field

Depth of field is an expression of the amount of a picture that is in clear sharp focus. If the entire picture is in focus with both near and far objects sharp in the same image then there is a large depth of field.

If one part of the image is in focus, say the central subject, but the foreground and the background are out of focus, then there is a narrow depth of field.

This is an inherent characteristic of the lens, but can also be influenced by the aperture setting.

The smaller the aperture the greater is the depth of field that will be achieved. Conversely, to deliberately throw the background out of focus you can open the aperture to its greatest setting.

Zoom lenses

These are lenses with a variable focal length. They are the mainstay of many photographic kits. They provide in a single lens an alternative to a range of prime lenses.

They do tend to use quite a bit of light so they are generally slow lenses. Faster ones are available but they are expensive. There is a lot of technology packed into one zoom lens and this does have its drawbacks.

Tools of the trade

These lenses can have the effect of slightly splitting light so that a hue is visible on the image and the colours are not quite true to life. Some manufacturers have overcome this problem, but at a cost. Some manufacturers have made a feature of colour correction. Sigma, for example, have come up with the APO range of lenses. This stands for apochromatic and means the lens has been corrected for this colour distortion. Conversely you could say that it is a recognition that their standard non-APO range distorts the colour. I have used these APO lenses and found them to be an excellent and less expensive zoom than the marque alternatives. The Sigma APO 70-300mm autofocus f4-5.6 is priced at £330 while the Nikon nearest equivalent, the 75-300mm autofocus f4.5-5.6 is on the market at £595. That's quite a difference in price to consider.

Zoom lenses cover a variety of different ranges. The greater the range a single lens covers, the more demands are made upon the technology. There comes a stage when an excessive range jeopardises quality and light usage. I recommend a series of zoom lenses so that with two or three lenses you can cover a huge scale.

These are the zooms I have chosen to use with my Nikon F4S, as my main camera outfit:

1. A Sigma lens that goes from 18-35mm - that's my wide and ultra-wide covered at a reasonable cost.
2. A Nikon lens that goes from 35-70mm - that covers the standard plus a little range on either side. I've chosen the marque lens here because it is one that I use a lot, but I compensated for the extra price by buying it secondhand.
3. A Nikon lens of 75-300mm - that covers the long range telephoto requirements.

So with just three lenses I have the option of focal lengths from 18mm to 300mm. None of these are very fast lenses but I have rarely found this to be a major drawback.

All you need to know about perspective

Everyone is familiar with the idea that things that are in the distance look small, and close up things loom large. We are also taught that parallel lines appear to converge as a function of their distance from the observer.

There is, however, a further aspect of perspective to consider; that of focus. We perceive the distance between objects by noting the difference in their sharpness of focus. If you hold your hand just in front of you and look at a distant object, your hand will go out of focus. Similarly if you focus on your hand, the distance will fall out of focus.

If this natural phenomenon is influenced by the optics of a lens, it is possible to confuse our perception of perspective.

A wide angle lens allows both near and far objects to be in focus at the same time. This broadens perspective and makes things look as though they are further away from each other than they actually are.

A long telephoto lens narrows perspective. The scene appears to be concertinaed. Objects appear to be much closer to each other than they actually are.

Filters

The camera is not quite as clever as the eye, and even the eye occasionally needs help in tricky lighting conditions. Nobody goes on holiday without a pair of sunglasses and using these darkened glasses is the equivalent of using a filter to enhance visibility.

There are many types of special effect filters that do things like turning specs of light into star bursts or putting rainbows in where they don't exist, but this is not really the sort of filter that I would consider to be part of the travel photographer's essential kit. There is always that need to keep the amount of equipment down to a bare minimum and filling your bags with an array of extraneous effects filters won't help. There are some filters, however, that I would consider invaluable. I would even go as far as to say that polarising filters are essential, but that any of the other filters are optional.

There are a number of different manufacturers of filters and like everything else, the products fall into a range of different prices. In general the better ones are more expensive although the cheaper ones

Lalibela Priest, Ethiopia - page 169

Morning Glory Pool, Yellowstone National Park, Wyoming, USA.- page 170

Piazza di Spagna, Rome - page 170

White-water Rafting - page 171

Black Bear, Alaska - page 172

Landscape Arch, Arches National Park, Utah, U.S.A.- page 173

Colossus of Ramses II, Abu Simbel, Egypt - page 174

may be adequate. If you spend a lot of money on lenses, choosing the ones that have the very best optical quality, your money is wasted if you then fit an inferior filter to the front of it. It will be like shooting through a window pane.

Filters come in different sizes that screw onto the front of the lens or as a single size that fits into a holder. The holder is then fitted with the appropriate adapter ring to fit a range of different sized lenses. This second type is usually the cheapest option in the long run. After you have bought the initial holder, you only need one of each type of filter. It is important to think of the biggest lens you have or are likely to get, in terms of physical diameter, when choosing a filter system.

I have made the mistake of having several different filters of the same type but of differing diameters to fit each of my lenses. At first this was the cheapest option but as I add more lenses of different diameters, I have to buy more filters. It is costly and bulky. As I consider expanding the range of filters that I want, I'm now considering the costs of starting all over again with an appropriate filter system. A little forethought would have saved me money.

Polarising filters

Polarising filters have a similar effect as sunglasses, although they work in a more precise and selective manner. They reduce glare and unwanted light that is bouncing about reflecting from non-metallic objects. Polarised light vibrates in one plane only, and by rotating a polarising filter you can selectively block out the glare from the desired planes.

Without the unwanted light you can see through things that would normally be blocked by reflective glare. Water surfaces and glass become transparent to reveal the deep colours or subjects behind them. It is a world without reflections.

One of the problems with glaring reflected light is that it affects the light metering systems inside the camera. The overall available light will be greater, so when the exposure is set for the average available light, the picture will have a loss of detail in the shadows and darker areas. By removing the glare, you increase colour saturation so that everything looks richer and of a deeper colour, as well as getting better details in the shadows. Reducing the available light results in the need to increase the exposure. You can do this either by using a wider aperture or by using a slower shutter speed.

There are two types of polarising filter: linear and circular. If you are using an autofocus lens, or any camera with a beam splitting device that determines exposure, you need a circular polariser. This is because the split beam will be affected by the polariser and the autofocus will not work, or the exposure settings will be inaccurate. These circular polarisers will also work on manual focus lenses so linear polarisers should be redundant. The only advantage of the linear polariser over the circular is that it is a little less expensive.

Warm-up filters

These are a range of filters which quite literally warm up the picture. Light naturally has the property known as colour temperature. This has nothing to do with air temperature and can be quite confusing. The appearance of light is warmer at sunrise and at sunset. It is that quality of a warm glow of light that relates to colour temperature. Stranger still is the way the measurement is expressed.

The kelvin scale (k) is used, which isn't odd in itself, but warm light has a low colour temperature and cool light has a high colour temperature. I don't know why simple concepts have to be expressed in such reverse logic; perhaps it is so that those who know what they are talking about can feel superior by baffling the newcomer with jargon. It annoys the hell out of me.

So a warm-up filter actually filters out high colour temperature and gives the effect of making the picture look warmer. It is perhaps easier to forget all about the kelvin scale and to think of blue as being cold and red as hot - just like colour codes for taps. If you want a blue scene to look a bit redder, then you use a warm-up filter.

The filter reduces hard blue casts that can occur at midday. It makes the orangey-brown things like buildings and rocks glow, just as they do in dawn and dusk lighting.

The filters come in a range of strengths. They are known as the 81 series filters, and range from 81A which has the mildest effect, to 81EF which has the strongest.

Graduated filters

A graduated filter has a strong effect at the top and reduces to no effect at the bottom. I have often found it difficult to get the right picture when the weather is not what I want it to be. Most markets want photos with bright blue skies but if you are only at a location for a day it might not be possible to get such a shot. Dark skies with lots of character can also sell, but anything with a bland sky just looks uninteresting. You can use colour filters to actually alter the image but this can sometimes look a little false. That artificial man-made look to a picture might have its place, but it's difficult to get it right and to find a market for it.

Grey filters can be used to darken an image without changing the actual colour of that image. If there is a grey cloudy sky that just makes the scene look dull a graduated grey filter will transform the picture. The foreground will still have all the light of the natural scene, but the grey portion of the filter carefully placed to mask the sky will make it look as though there is a storm brewing. A dramatic sky over a well-lit foreground can be a winning combination.

Compact cameras

Compact cameras are often thought of as point-and-shoot cameras. They are small and yet still capable of taking 35mm film which makes them an ideal travelling companion for the holiday photographer. The recent advances in their technology, however, have made them a serious and viable option for the travel photographer and not just the holiday-maker.

In general, compacts have only one fixed lens (there are a few exceptions). That limits the versatility of the camera but certainly doesn't make it useless. You always have the option to walk closer to or further away from an object! Joking apart, more and more of these compacts are developing zoom lenses that have an increased range of focal lengths.

The optical quality of these lenses can be rather poor and it's worth reading up on test results before buying one. They are always very slow lenses so they aren't much use in low light conditions.

Just about every function on these cameras is automatic and this does tend to make them a little gimmicky. Having said that, they have been an excellent testing ground for new automation technology and several things originally developed for compacts are now incorporated on the modern SLRs. The drawback of automation to this extent is that it relies on the camera interpreting the scene on the basis of averages. This can produce some very average photos. You don't have the option to manually over-ride the automation to get the picture *you* want to take.

As a compact is not a single lens reflex camera, the image in the viewfinder has not come through the lens that will be creating the picture. It has come through a separate finder lens, so you must know how to frame the picture within these limitations.

With all these limitations you might wonder why I even mention these compact cameras. The simple answer is that in certain situations they are brilliant. I never know when I'm going to spot a good photo and so I always like to have a camera with me. There are times when I simply don't want to lug a heavy, bulky camera bag around with me. It may simply be a matter of convenience or can be a question of unobtrusiveness.

There are always warnings about getting mugged in foreign lands. Walking about with expensive equipment hanging from your neck is simply asking for trouble. This isn't just in third world countries and poor areas. I was warned by one tour guide not to carry a camera bag in the heart of Rome! I hasten to add that occasionally advice has to be ignored.

So the compact is inconspicuous and eminently portable. If you are prepared to pay for a top-of-the-range model, many of the limitations have been considered and overcome by the manufacturers. The good ones incorporate a whole range of exposure modes that allow you to programme your requirements for each picture. The difficulty is trying to work out exactly what effect each of the modes has on the camera's settings. I'm sure some options are duplicated with the same settings going under different mode names. Once you have worked out how to use all these gimmicks, though, the camera does become quite versatile.

Samsung were the first to bring out a compact that has a zoom lens ranging from 38-140mm, called their ECX1. That is impressive for a compact and is the best you can hope for if you're just going to carry a fixed lens camera. It has a mass of technology packed into it which allows very accurate light metering and an over-the-top range of settings.

Many compacts, this ECX1 included, have a flash incorporated into the camera body which is also automatic. The flash similarly has a choice of settings according to your requirements, and some of them are quite good. They do tend to cause red-eye. This is due to the angle at which the flash is fixed. The light from it hits the subject's eyes and reflects from the back of the retina. The angle is such that the reflected light goes straight into the camera's lens and makes the subject look like an alien. Red-eye reduction functions don't solve the problem. They have a double flash. The first flash causes the subject's pupils to contract and the second flash is the one that is used to take the picture. With a reduced pupil there is less area for the light to reflect from the retina. People look like they have pin-hole eyes. The red-eye is reduced but not done away with. The first flash might also have inadvertently attracted people to look towards you just at the wrong moment so you can actually end up with more incidents of red-eye. You just can't sell this sort of photo so you have to make sure you don't take any photos with people looking directly at the camera.

I have found that the lens on this Samsung compact is so slow that it is impractical to use any film below 100 ISO which is a bit of a shame, but I've been able to take some excellent photos with it, both with and without the flash. It is a bit expensive at around £400, but when I'm using it, it's serving as a substitute for a complete camera outfit. When you add up the cost of an SLR, its lenses, perhaps a separate flash, filters, accessories and a bag in which to carry it all, the compact starts to look like good value.

If you really don't place as much importance on your photography as on your writing then this sort of point-and-shoot camera could do as your only camera. You could get away with using this and nothing else, but you would have to accept the limitations. The chances are that you would still get some very useable pictures, and certainly enough to chose from if you only want the occasional shot to accompany an article.

Tripods

The single piece of equipment that can improve picture quality more than anything else is a tripod. It can be quite difficult to get into the habit of always using a tripod for every shot, but it really is worth it. I always want to use slow film and that means long exposures. Even though most exposures only last for a fraction of a second the pictures suffer from minute movements known as camera shake.

Just using a tripod as a matter of course dramatically reduces camera shake and the results are spectacularly improved. There are drawbacks to using a tripod, such as drawing attention to yourself. People notice you setting the thing up and this can be a disadvantage for candid shots. Some photographs need immediacy and by the time you have set up the tripod and camera the moment can be lost. It's just a matter of using it most of the time, rather than all of the time.

The other slightly limiting factor is the weight of a decent tripod. It is yet another piece of equipment to be carted around and you can end up needing a pack horse for all this kit. You can make the effort, though, and the rewards are worthwhile. I remember dragging a tripod up an active volcano in Guatemala and wishing I had left it behind, but the photos I got of the eruption were stunning (front cover). There is no way I could have got these photos without a tripod.

When deciding which tripod to buy there are a couple of considerations. The tripod is not going to be used in a studio, but when you are on the move in all sorts of conditions. The ground it is to stand on will be uneven and could be at a very awkward angle. Versatility is therefore as important as portability. It needs to be robust in order to withstand the travelling and strong enough to support the camera, bearing in mind that the robust cameras that are needed can also be heavy pieces of equipment.

Some photography guides say that the cheap tripods are lightweight, portable and therefore ideal for travel photography. This is absolute rubbish. The cheap equipment is just that - cheap. It breaks and falls to pieces. It will not hold the weight of robust cameras and will certainly not put up with the wear and tear of travelling.

Benbo have addressed these issues and come up with an excellent design. Their range of tripods includes one called the Benbo Trekker. It really can be put up anywhere because of its ingenious articulating single bolt joint that allows the legs to be set in any direction. It is quite heavy but it will hold weighty equipment and it is certainly robust. It is a little on the expensive side but to my mind is the perfect choice for travelling.

Flash units

Some cameras, notably the compact cameras, have an integral flash - that is a flash which is incorporated into the body of the camera. Many of the mid-range SLR cameras also have an integral flash but they usually have the option to fit an external flash as well.

On the top of the camera body is a small socket known as a hot shoe. When a flash unit is connected to this it can communicate with the camera's internal electronics. There are dedicated flash units that are designed to be used with a specific camera. To be able to use all the functions that the camera is capable of, it may be necessary to buy the flash unit that is made by the camera's manufacturer. This is often the most expensive option, and not strictly needed.

Several manufacturers make flash units that are designed to work with all the different cameras. I use a modular system made by Centon which is a relatively inexpensive option.

This has a base module specifically for Nikon cameras or I can use a base unit specifically for Pentax, or whatever make I happen to choose. The base module has all the electronics that allow it to be compatible with the camera's electronics. The flash itself is a separate module that can be attached to the appropriate base units.

Compatibility is important for synchronisation and TTL (Through The Lens) metering. The synchronisation ensures that the flash goes off at the same time as the shutter opens and the picture is taken. To enable this to happen there is usually a maximum shutter speed that must be used with the flash. This flash synchronisation speed is sometimes automatically set; the camera uses this speed when it senses that a flash unit is actively connected to it. Other cameras have a flash setting that must be selected before the unit will synchronise.

When cameras use TTL light metering, the available light reading is taken by the camera through the lens. The calculation for the amount of flash light needed is transmitted between the flash unit and the camera via the hot-shoe. If the flash is incompatible with the camera these automatic settings will not be available. Even so, you can often manually set the flash but you do need the timing to be correctly synchronised. Some cameras do not have this TTL flash metering system anyway.

There is a scale known as the guide number (GN) which indicates the strength of the flash. The higher the number the greater the potential strength of output. Typically an integral flash will have a GN of about 12, but if you are buying an external unit it is worth getting one with a GN of about 30. All portable flash units, however, only have a small range.

There is a tendency for inexperienced photographers to overestimate the strength and capabilities of a flash. I have seen people with automatic cameras taking sunset shots. The flash goes off as though it has the capability to light the landscape scene all the way to the horizon. In fact these portable flash units will only light a few feet, or at best a few metres, in front of the camera. They can be very useful for fill-in flash. This is where you use flash as well as daylight. The flash gets rid of the shadows and brings out highlights, 'filling in' the detail in the dark parts of the scene.

Containers and cases

In every part of this section on tools of the trade I have mentioned how important it is to have robust equipment. The very nature of travel means that the equipment is likely to be exposed to harsh conditions and environments. However robust the things might be, though, they still need looking after. The risks and damage done can be greatly reduced by having suitable bags, containers and cases.

It is very easy to waste a great deal of money buying things that will not put up with travelling conditions. Luckily there are lots of cheap options which can be taken. The best place to find the cheap options is anywhere but in a camera shop. You just need to think in slightly broader terms than limiting yourself to conventional photographic cases, and you can think of a whole range of products that will do the same job for a fraction of the cost.

The basic things from which you need to protect your equipment are the environmental hazards like dust and water, and the physical damage caused by knocks and scrapes. This means that the containers need to be air tight, waterproof and physically protective.

The cheapest containers

Polythene bags:

Perhaps the single cheapest and most versatile piece of equipment is the humble plastic bag. My kit bag always includes a big black bin liner. If all else fails and I am caught unawares by a rain storm or unexpectedly have to take my camera bag onto a boat and am concerned it might get splashed, out comes the bin liner. The whole bag can be covered up and protected.

Smaller plastic bags are extremely useful for covering individual pieces of equipment when they are not being used. It is always important to make sure that things are put away dry in the first place or you could inadvertently seal moisture into equipment rather than keeping it out.

Plastic food boxes:

At the simplest, cheapest level I think food containers meet all the required criteria. They are airtight and watertight and afford an amount of physical protection. Those versatile plastic boxes are fairly inexpensive and come in a range of shapes and sizes. There are even cylindrical ones that make good lens cases. Packets of silica crystals are often found in boxes when you buy new equipment. These are very useful as they absorb water and dry the air within the microenvironment of the container. They can be dried out and re-used indefinitely. Packing equipment in plastic bubble-wrap adds still further protection against physical damage and the food containers themselves are quite strong and will put up with some heavy wear.

Obviously you can have as many of these containers as are needed and make up the set that suits the particular equipment that is to be protected. If these were marketed as camera accessories they would be sold as a modular system for versatile storage, protection and transportation and would cost five times the price. I personally prefer to think of them as 'tupperware' boxes.

Metal film canisters:

The film containers I use are even cheaper than plastic boxes; in fact they are free. When I buy bulk reels of film it comes in metal canisters. The particular brand I use comes on a two inch core which means that the container is larger than some of the others. These metal tins are basically waste, and yet they will hold twenty rolls of film. Sealed with a bit of electrical insulating tape they provide perfect storage. This is far less bulky than the traditional plastic pods that individual film come in. The canisters have the added advantage of being x-ray proof and therefore afford still further protection to film stock. Some people say that putting film into any kind of x-ray proof container only encourages the x-ray machine operators at airports to turn up the power to see inside them. The higher power presents a far greater risk than the unprotected film would have been exposed to. This is surely supposition and scaremongering - I have never had a film damaged inside these metal containers. There is, however, always a first time. I checked this out with a security guard at Houston airport when I was asked to physically open one of these canisters. It appears that there is no way the x-rays can penetrate these metal canisters.

Plastic tool boxes:

Sometimes it is easy to distribute the containers throughout my baggage, but sometimes I like to have it all packed away together. This is particularly useful for all that spare equipment that is taken along in case of theft. Most of the time it will not even be looked at if all goes well. If I'm travelling in a vehicle and have no problems with storage space, I put all the small food boxes together into a plastic tool box, pack it away and forget about it until the end of the trip.

Most hardware stores sell tough plastic tool boxes. They are light and strong and very cheap when compared with the alternatives. They are not waterproof but the lids fit quite well and keep out all but the most persistent dust.

Specialist cases

One thing I have an aversion to is aluminium boxes. Sure, they are lightweight and they are tough and hard-wearing. It is fair to say that they are well designed and come in a range of sizes and many are specifically aimed at the photography market.

To me the drawback is their popularity. They lack subtlety and you might as well put a big label on them saying "this box contains valuable equipment". I've seen these boxes at the baggage reclaim carousels at airports. It amazes me that they have arrived at all and I certainly wonder if their contents are still complete.

Baggage really isn't safe on an aircraft. I once checked a bag in at a British Airways desk and when it arrived back in England it had been rifled and a camera had been stolen. It was in a discreet, grubby-looking bag, so the risk would have been even higher if I had put all my equipment in a shiny aluminium box.

There are a number of tough plastic cases that have been specially designed to store sensitive and fragile equipment. Some claim to be unbreakable which is perhaps a little over the top, but they are certainly strong. They have an O-ring seal that guarantees a watertight seal and are therefore also dust proof and airtight. Most have a choice of inserts which allow you to customise the protective packing to your own needs. These boxes are excellent. Their only drawback is that they are expensive.

Camera bags

There are quite literally hundreds of different camera bags available. These can be very expensive items but are absolutely essential. The hard cases and boxes are all very well for transportation and storage, but you can't actually walk about with all your kit in these. The camera bag is for all the things you might want to use on a particular day.

The size and shape of a bag is a matter of personal choice, and it depends on the particular equipment you want to carry around. The practicality of the design is one thing to look at. The bag doesn't just have to be able to hold the kit and afford it a certain amount of protection, it also has to be user-friendly. It needs pockets and compartments so that all things are easily accessible. It can be infuriating having to unpack the whole bag because some small piece of kit has made it to the bottom of the bag.

I have had camera bags in the past that are absolute dust traps. They seem to attract dust rather than exclude it. On some bags, which are not necessarily cheap, the zips and fasteners don't put up with constant use, and the straps come away from the bags.

I personally like the Billingham bags. They are used by many professional photographers quite simply because they are one of the best range of bags on the market. They are extremely well made, using leather and brass fittings and very strong straps. The bag itself is made of layers of hard-wearing canvas that incorporate a waterproofing layer. There are lots of flaps covering the openings to the different compartments so that even if the bag gets splashed or rained on, water will not drip through the zips. They are pricey but could well outlive you so it is money well spent.

Secondhand equipment

I have mentioned a few tools of the trade which I feel can quite happily be bought on the secondhand market, notably word processors and camera bodies. I do think this is a viable option especially when just starting up. There are some things to think about though, and to look out for on this market.

If you are VAT registered you are not able to reclaim the tax on secondhand equipment as you would be able to on new equipment. This could amount to a considerable sum and might mean that there is little difference between the actual cost of new and old.

Anything you buy from a private advertisement has absolutely no guarantee with it. The equipment might look fine, but what happens if it goes wrong? I would avoid this section of the secondhand market like the plague.

When you are buying computers you might be very glad of the backup services that tend to come only with new equipment. I bought my secondhand computer from a friend who knew a great deal more about the subject than I did at the time. He was happy to guarantee it and to give me free backup. There were a few teething problems which were largely as a result of my lack of experience rather than a fault with the equipment, but true to his word, he popped round and sorted things out for me. This is fine if you buy from a trustworthy friend, but I would be concerned buying something from the small ads from an unknown source. Who do you turn to when you get stuck?

For secondhand photographic equipment I would also be wary of private sales unless I knew the photographer. It is important to try to ascertain why the kit has been sold by its previous owner. Just going to a dealer doesn't necessarily solve your problems. There are several reputable dealers and hundreds of less reliable ones. Some companies that guarantee secondhand camera equipment are relying on statistical probabilities. A guarantee doesn't mean that something won't be faulty, simply that if it is faulty it will be repaired free of charge. It is a calculated risk on their part and at worst they may have to replace the item or refund your money. That isn't much help to you if you have gone off travelling or if the fault doesn't show up until the photos are developed.

Any camera equipment that has been used professionally may have been subject to considerable wear. This is not obvious and indeed often not visible. A camera used in a studio might have been used to take 100 rolls of film a day for several years. Every single moving part is subject to wear and you have no idea how close it is to breaking. Reputable dealers are far better judges of condition and usually know what the camera has been used for. They judge the market price accordingly and put their own reputation behind the sale as well as their guarantee.

If you buy a Nikon from Grays of Westminster, for example, you are on to a fairly safe bet. Other dealers, such as Jessop's, reflect their stance by the terms they offer - they will not sell you an extended guarantee on professional equipment. They send requested items from branch to branch via a central office so that in the end the person selling the equipment may have absolutely no idea of where or how it has been used by its previous owner. It is an excellent service for tracking down things that you want, but I am not sure what would happen if you find that something is worn out after the first six months, which is all their guarantee covers. In this case being known as a professional goes against you - any equipment bought by a professional will not be offered the extended guarantee. Quite logically, they can see the risks involved with constant use, but it seems a bit one-sided if you can't find out about previous owners.

Some dealers seem to have no idea of what they are selling and have vastly differing standards when it comes to 'good condition'. Others, like my local shop Anglia Cameras in Ipswich, have a very clear idea of standards. The small shops tend to have a more limited selection and are sometimes a little more expensive, but their service can be worth a great deal. I find that nothing is too much trouble for them. They know the history of the equipment because they know their customers, and they are always happy to give advice.

Chapter 6

Film

Photography is a bit like cooking; you have to have all the right ingredients to get the best results. It doesn't matter how much care you take in composing your picture or what camera equipment you use to take it, if the film isn't right you won't get the best results. There are a lot of different films and it can be a bit of a minefield finding out the difference between them. As film is retailed at chemists, kiosks and supermarkets you can't rely on the retailers knowing anything about the films they are selling.

Slides or prints?

This is dictated by the market. Many publications claim that they will get better reproduction quality from slides than they will from prints. The technology is such that this is not necessarily the case, but if they won't buy prints you have to sell them slides.

Picture libraries generally only take slides. Magazines, books and newspapers also generally insist on slides.

The Daily Telegraph have taken the initiative to have all their commissioned work taken on prints. They know you can look at a big print much more easily than at a small slide and have no fear of the technology to produce good results.

Until others follow this example, however, there is absolutely no question of the freelance taking anything but slides.

You must take slides.

Film speed

The speed of the film is the all-important characteristic. The light-sensitive part of the film is an emulsion of chemicals that coats one side of the film. The speed of the film is represented by the ISO number and is the speed at which the chemical emulsion reacts to light.

Quite apart from the different chemistry, slower films have emulsions that are physically thicker. Light hits the film and slowly burns its way into this thick layer of emulsion. The result is a far richer picture than that taken on a fast film with a thin emulsion.

So the slower the film, the deeper and richer are the colours. They have greater colour saturation. The drawback with slow films is that you need either more light or a longer exposure time for a given amount of light. 'More light' is achieved by a wider lens aperture, whilst longer exposures are achieved by a slower shutter speed.

Slow films also have a much finer grain. This enables them to be blown up to far greater sizes with a minimal loss of quality. Fast grainy films can make for interesting effects but have a more limited market.

If you are trying to freeze something in motion then you need a fast film. For stationary objects, like a landscape, you can stick the camera on a tripod and take as long as you want, so a slow film is fine. Low light levels, such as those I've experienced under the jungle canopy of a rainforest, don't lend themselves to slow films. Faster lenses let you use slower films but they cost so much money. It is thus always a play-off between quality, practicality and the capabilities of the equipment being used.

I always use the slowest possible film that I can get away with so that I don't lose quality. I do occasionally get caught out, however, finding myself in a situation where the light levels are low and I have only got a 50 ISO speed film in the camera. Whatever you intended your subject and light conditions to be, it is worth having a selection of films of differing speeds in your camera bag, just in case they are needed.

All you need to know about uprating and push processing

This is a method of using a film with one ISO rating as a film of another ISO rating. You have to use the whole film like this, not just a single shot on it. You quite simply adjust the ISO setting on the camera to the required speed and then tell the processing house that the film has been uprated. It can then be "push processed" to compensate for this effect with quite reasonable results.

If you only have 100 ISO film with you but need something faster you can just set the camera to 200 ISO. Doubling the speed is known as uprating by one stop. Taking a 100 ISO film with the camera set at 400 would therefore be uprating by 2 stops. It then has to be push processed by 2 stops.

Film brands

To an extent the brand you use comes down to a matter of personal choice. You will find one photographer is a big fan of Agfa while another prefers Kodak. I personally like the results I get from Fuji.

One type I would always avoid is home brands of film. There is often nothing wrong with these films but you just don't know what you are buying. The large retailers buy a bulk order of film from the cheapest source and have it packaged under their own house brand name. It could well be film that has come from one of the top manufacturers, but, as each brand has slightly different characteristics to its end colour results, I like to know exactly what I'm buying, not just how much it costs.

It is interesting to look through a few photography magazines and independent books. Many of the published photos have details of the type of film that the photographer used. A very high proportion of them use Fuji and in particular Fuji Velvia. Some of the photo libraries, and indeed even some picture editors for individual publications, stipulate that they prefer images taken on Fuji Velvia.

It is certainly my preferred film and at 50 ISO is one of the slowest on the market. It gives excellent rich colour saturation. It makes the images look very bold and sometimes gives them more colour than they actually have in real life. This gives the image lots of visual impact and makes it more likely to sell.

Both Agfa and Kodak make extremely good films that have the reputation of producing colours that are far more true to life. They are used by many professional photographers so I would reiterate that it is partly a question of personal choice. It is far more important to consider the film speed rather than the brand.

Bulk film

Several retailers will give a discount for buying films in bulk - usually ten or more rolls. There is, however, a far cheaper way of buying film: you can buy it on bulk reels. Instead of rolls of 24 or 36 shots you can buy it as a single roll of 100 feet (30.5 metres).

You then have to buy the empty cassettes and load them yourself with the desired length of film. 100 feet rolls up to 20 films of about 36 shots.

This does have to be carried out with extreme caution. The bulk roll of film has to be opened in total darkness or the entire thing will be ruined. I have done it in a small room with the window blacked out but a proper dark room would be better if available.

The individual lengths can be rolled up by hand. You cut off the required length, attach it to the centre core of the cassette and roll it up. Then you have to put on the outer casing and seal it up. All this is quite difficult in total darkness and extremely time consuming. The alternative is to buy a bulk film loader. These aren't very expensive and make the job a lot easier.

The bulk roll still has to be loaded into loader itself in complete darkness. A compartment reveals the loose end of the film which you attach to the cassette. You close the compartment and wind on the film with a little handle. There is a counter to show how many shots you have wound on and in theory this can all be carried out without being in darkness.

It's a bit nerve racking because you don't know if you have

inadvertently let light get at the film. If this is the case you haven't just wasted one film but potentially ruined a whole batch of 20. You won't know till you come back from your travels and get the films processed.

I've never had this go wrong, but I do take the added precaution of using the loader in complete darkness.

The whole point of this exercise is that the film ends up costing you about half what it would cost at a discounted retail price. It is just a matter of time and confidence. The cassettes are blank so it is quite important to label them.

DX codes

DX codes are information labels that are encoded onto the outside of film cassettes. They look like a pattern of silver and black boxes. This code contains the ISO number (film speed) of the film and can be read by most modern cameras with a DX coding function. The idea is that your ISO number is automatically set and you don't have to set it manually each time you change the type of film you load into the camera. This is intended to reduce the risk of incorrect exposures due to forgetting to set the speed.

Like any automatic system it has its drawbacks. Some cameras don't have a manual override system so you are forced to use the film at its intended ISO setting and don't have the option to uprate the film.

If you have bulk film that you loaded yourself, the cassettes do not carry this important DX information. You can, however, buy DX labels and stick them on. These can be obtained through Jessop's but they do add a few pence to the overall cost of each film. You could also use these labels to override a DX coding on a film by sticking the appropriate code over the existing one.

Professional films

Some films are marketed as 'professional film'. I'm not sure if this means that the other films in the same manufacturer's range aren't very good at being films.

Fuji make a range of films that they call Provia. These are far more expensive than their other range, called Sensia, but are apparently more suitable for the professional. I asked Fuji what the difference was. The emulsion, they told me, is exactly the same. The Provia, however, has been bulk aged. This gives consistency between rolls. I suppose if you were taking lots of rolls of the same subject this could be a consideration. For my kind of photography, though, I fail to see how this bulk aging does anything but cost me money.

One travel photographer I heard give a lecture advised "never use a film marked professional", but I certainly don't agree with this sweeping statement. His reasoning was that professional films are more sensitive, have a smaller shelf life and require more careful storage. You have to keep them in a fridge which isn't very practical if you are a travel photographer on the move.

I notice that rolls of Fuji Velvia are marked as 'for professionals' (which makes a bit more sense of the expression) and the bumph recommends that they are stored in a refrigerator at 15°C or lower. That might be the best thing to do in an ideal world, but all I can say is that I have never had any problem with this film. I have taken films on long trips where there just aren't any storage facilities and they have had to put up with the high temperatures of deserts or tropical climates week after week. I have never detected any deterioration, but there is always a first time.

Chapter 7

Presentation

You may have written a masterpiece and illustrated it with the most stunning photographs of the highest quality, but if you cannot present this to your customer in a way that makes him want to look at it you will fall at the first fence.

By considering writing and photography together there is an underlying acceptance of the need for visual impact. Indeed I have already mentioned the fact that many magazines are becoming ever more picture orientated.

Whether approaching a newspaper or magazine editor, a book publisher or any other of the numerous markets for our product it is important to realise that all these people are customers. As customers they are influenced by exactly the same things as the readers who in turn buy their product. If they feel that visual impact sells their publication then they will want to buy something that similarly has visual impact.

Presentation is about the initial appearance of a submission rather than the content or quality of the product itself. If it looks good there is every chance that it will at least be considered.

A couple of months ago someone sent me a few travel articles that they had written, asking for my advice and any tips I might have on selling the pieces. The letter was hand written on a piece of A4 with holes punched down one side. It had obviously been written in a great hurry and had not even been looked at, let alone read through. It had crossings out and extremely poor punctuation such as brackets, slashes, dashes and some plus signs that glared up from the page even before I had read the words.

The articles looked as though they had been fed through a fax machine instead of a photocopier. The result was that the articles were reproduced on a roll of fax paper which had poorly copied both the type and the image of the punched holes from the original. This nasty, shiny, flimsy paper was then unevenly cut and torn into page lengths and stapled together. Odd lines had gone missing and had been scribbled back in with a ballpoint. There were little scrappy drawings and notes inserted in the text and still more crossings out and notes in the margins.

The whole package of thirteen foolscap pages, a business card and a return envelope were folded together and stuffed into an envelope. The paper size didn't fit the envelope so it had to be folded in quarters and then the ends bent over. The stuffed package was so full that the envelope would not seal and had to be secured with tape. She chose to use a rather grubby looking piece of masking tape.

The result was a package that arrived at my door looking visually very unattractive. If I was a potential customer the whole thing might well have gone in the bin. Some editors do claim that they will read anything, however it is presented, but I am quite sure most would have been tempted to return this package in the envelope provided.

Personally I was fascinated that anyone should send something out in such a state. I may not be a potential customer for this work, but it brought home to me the importance of good presentation. Customer or not, these things are noticed.

I resolved that nothing should ever leave my desk without the presentation being considered. I ask myself what the initial impact will be when the package is received and opened at its destination.

Presenting the writing - The manuscript

There are a few aspects of presentation that are generally accepted within the industry. Although there are no standards that have to be adhered to 100%, I can see no reason to ignore the norms and run the risk of instant rejection. Despite my derogatory comments about the presentation of that package someone sent to me, at least the articles were correctly typed and double spaced.

What we are trying to do is put words on paper in an easily readable manner. It does not have to be overtly attractive, but it must not be off-putting. Initially you might think that there is little to consider here, after all there is only the paper and the words. I have discovered that there are innumerable variables within those two categories and it is extremely important to consider them carefully. Despite the ease with which documents can be down-loaded onto a floppy disk and transferred directly onto another computer, most editors still like to see a hard copy of the work - a paper manuscript. Here are some of the starting points:

- All manuscripts, whether for short articles, fill-ins or entire books, should be typed.
- There is no need to go for fancy, expensive, heavy or coloured papers. Plain white 80gm, A4 paper is the norm. (See notes on paper)
- The text should be typed on one side of the paper only.
- The text should be double spaced.
- There should be an adequate margin at both sides of the text as well as above and below.

I am not suggesting that articles will be rejected by not following any one of these points, but together they make up a good sensible way of presenting your work. These are all fairly simple, basic points which will lead to a neat manuscript that is easily read. The reader can clearly see all the words and is not put off by scrappy paper or illegible handwriting.

Line spacing

Line spacing is the distance between two lines of text. Single spacing places one line immediately under another. Double spacing, or double line spacing as it is sometimes called, is the term used for leaving a gap equivalent to one line of text between each of the lines of written text. In effect, you write on every other line. This paragraph is double spaced.

All you need to know about paper

Paper comes in various **sizes** which are represented by 'A' numbers.
The common ones are:

A3 is 297mm x 420mm

A4 is 210mm x 297mm - which is half a piece of A3

A5 is 148mm x 210mm - which is half a piece of A4 or a quarter of a piece of A3

A4 comes as close to being a standard as we get in the UK. Foolscap, legal, letter and executive are other common sizes which may be used within a particular profession or by other countries.

A single page of a magazine is usually A4 sized - so a double page spread is A3. This is worth knowing if you are trying to photocopy a two page article as most photocopiers have a choice of A3 or A4 paper in their trays.

Paper comes in different **weights**.

The weight of a paper is known as the gram weight. This is because it is measured in terms of grams per square metre which is expressed by the letters gsm or occasionally shortened to just 'g'.

The commonest papers for photocopiers and computer printers is **80gsm**. Heavier papers are sometimes used for letters and high quality presentations. They are often referred to as premium paper and are 85, 90 or even 100gsm.

Computer paper with holes down each side is designed to run through continuous feed printers as a continuous sheet. It is perforated and can be separated into individual sheets after printing. It is generally a much lighter, flimsier paper of about 60 or 70gms known as listing paper. You can, however, buy a high quality 90gsm micro-perforated paper if you have a printer with this system of feed and want a quality presentation.

Quantities: A **ream** is 500 sheets

So if you want to buy some ordinary paper you will probably get a ream of A4 80gsm plain white paper.

Presentation

There are a couple of reasons for double spacing text. Your manuscript not only presents your piece for consideration, but, once accepted, it becomes a working document. Even in this day and age the actual piece of paper you send in will be used to produce the final published work. Someone needs to copy the words into a computer to typeset them. If it is clearly laid out then there is less chance of mistakes being made. If text is too compact the copy typist may inadvertently miss out a whole line. This double spaced format also allows room for amendments to be clearly made to the text. You might be happy with the work that you send in, but an editor may need to change it slightly. This could be simply the fact that they have to fit the piece into a given space of their publication and need to reduce the length by a few words. The editor's pen can crop sections, cross out words or phrases and make notes in the text. This white space within the text gives room for this to be done without reducing the document to a cramped mess. The copy typist can still clearly make out the new amended version and quickly transfer it for type setting.

How to produce double line spacing on a word processor

Word processing packages are all different and even the different numbered versions are different from each other as they are improved and modified. Somewhere on the system you use, however, there will be a facility which enables you to produce double line spacing. Below are some examples of windows-run programmes that I have had a look at. You may have a different version so do not take these instructions as gospel, they are intended only as a guide and as examples.

There are some very simple programmes, such as **Write,** which you automatically get when you buy Microsoft Windows. When writing a document, there is a function heading 'Paragraph'. If you select this you are given a choice of single space, 1½ space, or double space. Select double space.

More complex word processing packages such as Microsoft **Word**, Lotus **Ami Pro** or its successor **WordPro** are more versatile. You can change marked blocks of text to double line spacing or create an entirely new style that will automatically write in double line spacing.

There is a line of commands under the heading of 'Format' for Word or 'Text' for Ami Pro that lead you to the choice of spacing. This allows a highlighted block to be changed.

To create a new style that writes in double line spacing you just have to follow a slightly different line of commands. In Ami Pro you start with 'Style' and follow on with 'Create New' whereas with Word you start with 'Format' and follow on with 'Style' and then 'New'.

Another group of word processors is the desk top publishing programmes. These tend to use words that are more commonly associated with the printing industry than with home computing. **PageMaker** uses the word **Leading** (pronounced 'ledding') as another way of expressing the line spacing.

When setting up styles, or indeed selecting the available functions under the heading 'Type', there is a heading marked Leading. This will adjust the line spacing. If writing in 12 point size text then selection of 24 point leading gives something akin to double spacing.

Correcting mistakes

Work should never be sent out without it being checked over. At this final stage small mistakes are often picked up that were missed earlier. It could be something simple like a comma missed out, a duplicated word or a word missing, or it could be that you decide a phrase just isn't right.

Crossing things out on an otherwise finished manuscript looks bad. It destroys the image or neatness and tidiness that helps make the piece easily readable and therefore more saleable.

It is extremely easy to re-open the file on a word processor and make the correction. The individual page can then be reprinted. Sometimes the correction changes the whole layout, pushing some text over to the next page. If this happens then just reprinting one page will leave a sentence or two incomplete.

Sometimes it is just not practical to reprint an entire document. I do make changes by hand occasionally, particularly if a manuscript is lengthy or if I'm in a hurry to meet a deadline and about to miss the post. At least with the double line spacing there is room to make the corrections without entirely destroying the look of the document. I always avoid hand-written corrections, however, if I am approaching any potential customer, such as an editor, for the very first time. I would rather delay sending things out than have them go out looking a mess when I'm trying to make an impression with a new contact.

All you need to know about type faces

Bold, *Italic* and Normal are three different ways in which a piece of text may be printed. There are, however, many different **fonts** to which these may be applied. Each font is a different and distinctive form of lettering as individual as a person's handwriting. These fonts are given all sorts of strange names. The commonly used ones are Times New Roman, Arial, and Courier New. There are an endless number of exotic ones such as **ALGERIAN**, Benguiat Frisky and *Phyllis*. Each of these in turn can be altered to print in italics or bold.

A **Serif** is a line at the end of each stroke of a type character that finishes them off. For example this is an "r" with a serif and this is an "r" without. This type face is a serif type face, whilst this is a sans serif (without serif).

A **True Type**™ font is a font that can be manipulated in terms of size without losing its distinct characteristics and can be transmitted to and recognised by a printer in that form. What you see on the screen is exactly the same as what will be printed. Type fonts without this characteristic require the printer as well as the computer to be programmed with the font; otherwise it will either not print, or an interpretation of it will be printed that is not true to type and may be quite different to what appears on the screen.

Most word processing packages have so many different type faces and styles that it can be quite difficult to decide what to use. It can be fun being creative and using different types for different applications but there is a danger of over-doing things. Good presentation of a manuscript should be simple and easy to read. It is best not to use more than two different type faces on a single page or it will all become a bit messy. For emphasis you are better to use the underline, bold or italic tools than to switch in and out of different fonts.

Justification

On bad days I wonder if the whole travel writing and photography career is worth the time and effort I spend on it for the low returns. Finding good reason and vindication, however, is nothing to do with justifying my text.

Justification, in terms of text presentation, is about adjusting the spaces between individual letters and between words so that a line of text fits neatly into a given space. This produces straight margins without white space at the ends of each line. Newspaper columns do it and so do many magazines and most books.

Word processors allow this function to be done quickly and simply, but when should it be used? There seem to be absolutely no definitive rules about text justification. One source says always justify your text, another says never justify. I therefore think it is only a matter of personal preference, and it is up to the individual to decide which looks better. The pages of this book are justified, but to illustrate the difference this paragraph is not.

Identifying Pages

It is quite possible for a manuscript to be dropped on the floor and someone then has to pick it up and reassemble the loose sheets in the right order. The first page of text usually has the title on it although this is not strictly necessary as there should be a cover sheet. Subsequent pages should be marked with a page number. The last page should have the word 'End' at the end of the text. This looks a bit like a school essay written by a child who puts 'The End' as a triumph of achievement, but it does serve a purpose. Quite simply the reader will know not to look for continuing sheets.

It is also possible that individual sheets become separated from each other. To avoid confusion it might be worth making sure each is identifiable as belonging to a particular manuscript; perhaps by putting the title or your initials on each page.

Front Page

The front page, cover sheet, or title page of any manuscript should say what it is and who it's by. Certain things should always be included and some are optional. There is a lot of white space on a cover sheet so that the information is clear and succinct.

Essentials:
- I always include a title even if the publication is likely to use a different one.
- The number of words - rounded to a suitable approximation.
- The writer's name and address

Options:
- It is a good idea to say what area the article is about if it is not obvious from the title.
- The name and address of the commissioning editor and publication that the piece has been written for.
- The rights being offered.

Example of a typical cover sheet:

```
          TITLE OF ARTICLE
   AN ARTICLE ABOUT TOWN/COUNTRY
        OF APPROX 1000 WORDS
               by


            GUY MARKS

       First British Serial Rights


         Commission No.123
           Prepared for:

              Name
            Travel editor
            A magazine
          Magazine House
              London

            Guy Marks
  Home Cottage, Home Lane, The Village, England
           Telephone.......
```

Bindings and Covers

Bindings and covers is another of those areas that is partly down to personal choice. I really don't believe that a piece of writing will be rejected just because it is bound in a way that the editor doesn't like. Having said that, you need to know what editors usually prefer so that you can make an informed decision.

Once the manuscript is all typed and printed you have a handful of loose sheets. Most editors prefer the pages not to be bound in any way. It is quite normal to clip them together with a paper clip but staples aren't particularly favoured.

Because of this aversion to binders, if I do want to use one, I use the type that have a clip holding in the pages. This way anyone can unclip the pages if they really find they want to look at them separately. This allows ease of handling when the article is accepted and someone has to copy type the text - single pages are easier to clip onto a typist's board.

In general I don't clip the pages together, I just put them in a simple open-sided clear plastic folder.

All you need to know about envelopes

There are a range of sizes of envelopes that directly relate to paper size. A huge amount of money can be wasted by buying the wrong stationery. There is nothing quite as infuriating as finding you have 125 board-backed envelopes that are just too small!

DL takes a piece of A4 paper folded into thirds.
C5 takes a piece of A4 paper folded in half.
C4 takes a piece of A4 paper unfolded.

To enable your work to be presented in pristine condition it may be worth sending it in full size board-backed envelopes that are big enough to take the work unfolded. Folders for A4 paper and slide sheets **are larger than the A4 work they contain** and may not fit into the C4 envelopes. Custom sizes are then required according to the dimensions of the presentation package.

All you need to know about postage

Whether you are sending out articles, photographs, or both, you should include return postage and perhaps even a return addressed envelope. It may seem a little one-sided but it is an essential of the business.

Whatever the publication they will be getting hundreds, if not thousands, of submissions and if you don't include the postage they may not return your work. Worse still is that they may not even reply to your proposal or inquiry if you do not include an s.a.e.

It may not bother you not to get the paper returned as you can print off another copy of the article, but laser prints cost real money and risking not getting a reply is pointless.

Photographs should always be sent by recorded or registered post. They are worth a lot of money and things *do* go missing. If you want them returned the same rules apply - include the return amount for registered or recorded delivery.

Presenting the photographs

I heard Frank Barrett, travel editor of the Mail on Sunday, say that the bad presentation of photographs was one of his pet hates. He told of opening envelopes on the train and finding masses of bits of paper, loose slides and photos tumbling out of the packets to find some dark resting place on the carriage floor. This is not where I want my precious work to end up.

Just from its size and the fact that it doesn't need a light source, a print is obviously a lot easier to look at than a slide. One problem is that a packet of prints will inevitably end up going missing or falling on the carriage floor. The other problem is that most of the work that I do is on slide. There is a note about the need to produce your work as transparencies on page 103.

Physical presentation of slides

Nobody is likely to bother to take slides out of a box, load them into a rack or carousel and project them onto a screen just to make a selection. If slides are sent in a box they probably won't even get looked at if there is an alternative source of supply.

I send out slides in clear plastic **slide sheets**. There are a whole range of different makes at different prices. The main consideration is that the slides should be easily viewable.

A clear sheet of slides can be placed on a light box in its entirety and viewed with the aid of a lupe (magnifying glass). Experienced picture editors can sift through hundreds of photos in a few moments. They home in on the ones that immediately catch their eye rather than scrutinising every shot on the sheet.

The most common sheets hold twenty 35mm slides. That means that twenty images can be looked at in an instant.

There is a huge difference in price of the different makes. It is not necessarily the case that the cheapest are the ones to use. Slides can and do fall out of these sheets and can easily get lost. Some of the sheets stretch and tear with very little use. Some are not archival quality plastic and damage may be done to the image if left in these plastics for long periods.

Within these sheets that hold the slides in groups of twenty, every single slide needs to be identifiable. Each slide needs a caption and the name of the copyright owner.

All you need to know about image format.

Format is the word used to express the physical size of an image. It refers to the image size at its point of creation, i.e. the size of the negative or the transparency.

The larger the format, the greater is the potential quality of any print produced from this initial image.

Standard film format is referred to as 35mm. This measurement is derived from the length of the longest side of the image.

Medium format images are 6×4.5cm, 6×6cm, 6×7cm or 6×9cm depending on the actual camera that is used. These cameras use 120 or 220 roll film.

Large format images are 5×4 or 10×8 inches.

Medium and large format cameras are bulky and expensive, so I am using 35mm as the standard for the travel photographer - see chapter 5 for 'Tools of the trade'.

Surma tribal people, Mursi Hana, Omo region of Ethiopia - page 175

Colours and textures: textiles in Guatemala and sand dunes in Morocco
- page 175

Erg Chebbi, Morocco - page 176

Moreno Glacier, Argentina - page 176

Templo de las Inscripciones, Palenque, Mexico - page 176

Inti Raymi at Sacsayhuamán ruins, Peru - page 177

London telephone box - page 177

Roof of St George's church, Lalibela, Ethiopia - page 178

Image identification

The simplest way to mark a slide is to get a rubber stamp made. For a couple of pounds I got one that reads '© Guy Marks'. I use a stamp pad with a quick-drying permanent ink; this 'takes' on the plastic mounts and dries so quickly that there is little chance of it smudging onto the transparencies.

It is possible to put the image caption onto a small label and stick it onto the slide mount. There are computer labelling systems available which will make this easier and neater. Personally I find this small space limiting and so I prefer the simple approach of putting just a reference number on a label on the mount.

Having just my **name** and a **reference number** on the slide means I have to enclose a separate **list of the captions**. This list is done in the same order as that in which the slides are arranged in the slide sheet. There is unlimited space on a list to put descriptions, captions, or any extra information about the image that might be of interest which would be impossible on a small label.

There is one more essential document that needs to be sent out with the slides. It is not really a matter of presentation but needs mentioning here just in case this chapter is being used as a check list. I send a **Delivery Note** which gives all the information about terms and conditions that apply to the offer of the images. These can be obtained from BAPLA (British Association of Picture Libraries and Agencies) who are happy to sell the forms to non-members.

Should slides be sent?

One of the major concerns is that photographs go missing. If at all possible I avoid sending out originals and this at least minimises the risk of losing the image forever. It is worth considering whether the potential customer actually needs to see the originals or if it is economically viable to send duplicates. Sometimes sending a laser print is even better than sending a slide. It all depends on the particular market and indeed to what stage of play the sale has progressed.

Slide libraries

A slide library will want to see the actual pictures that are being offered. They normally have strict instructions about presentation and will happily issue guideline notes. These include details of labelling and captioning requirements. As each library is different it is worth finding out this information before submitting work.

Photographic commissions

When I am approaching a company that I think might want the services of a photographer, such as a tour operator or tourist board, there is no need to send original slides. Most of the people looking at these images only want to get an idea of the sort of work I have done in the past. From this they can clearly see the style and quality of my work.

I send them a mixture of press cuttings of previously published work taken from magazines and travel brochures. Newspaper reproduction is often black and white and can be of poor quality so cuttings from these are less impressive. There is no point in sending in anything that does not make the work look really good. If I want to show a wide range of styles and topics I will also enclose some duplicate slides - making clear that they are duplicates.

Photographic submissions to publications

Sometimes I offer photographs without text, in response to a photo editor's request. Having found out that they need a certain topic I want to make sure that my work is considered. These requests or wants lists are usually for immediate or immanent publication. There is not time to send out examples or ask them to make choices from duplicates that are not of publishable reproduction quality. These customers require the actual slides from which they can make the reproduction.

Very high quality duplicate slides can be made for relatively little money per image. These are adequate for lots of the markets but it is worth checking first. Book editors may hold onto slides for many months, if not more than a year, and in this case it is particularly useful not to have sent the original. Hopefully there will be opportunities for other sales within that time.

The illustrated article

I have already pointed out the fact that pictures and text sell best together regardless of whether the package is photo-led or word-led.

If an article is being sent into a publication on spec, it is not practical to include *all* the photos at this early stage. Sometimes it is enough to say that photos will be available on request. This is often adequate if the editor knows my work; he knows that there really will be suitable photos available and doesn't have to see them up front. This, however, is not using the visual impact of the photos to help sell the work.

Making a list of photographs may help to give the editor an idea of the range of illustrations available but I have never known a selection to be made from a list alone; again, this is not making best use of the images as a sales tool. You are not wasting time in preparing this list, though, as the intention is to sell the article. At some stage the slides will indeed need to be sent out, and the list with the captions and slide reference numbers will make it easy to look out the slides from the files when the time comes.

Given that any piece will probably have about 20 possible photographs to illustrate it, there is a great deal of expense involved in getting duplicate slides made. More often than not, only one or two images actually get used with the piece and if the cost of twenty dupes has to be met there will be little left by way of profit. The package may sit around for a very long time before it is accepted or rejected and during that time you may deem it worthwhile to submit the piece to more than one potential market. Again, this makes it impractical to have numerous sets of duplicates going out on spec.

The ideal alternative to slides is the use of **laser prints**. Many instant print shops, which you find in nearly every town, have the machinery to produce these. A 35mm slide is placed in a projection mechanism which is part of a laser print copier - a colour photocopier. The image is scanned and a laser photocopy is produced instantly.

These laser prints are of extremely good quality although in my experience they do not match up to an actual print from slide or the quality of magazine reproduction. Their big advantage is that they are printed out on A4, so the image is large. There is often a setting-up charge plus a charge per copy. This is expensive if only one copy is required but by looking ahead to potential articles I can usually find several slides that I want to get printed at the same time. This reduces the cost to a reasonable expense. I always print a note on the back of the laser copy to the effect that the image is available as a 35mm transparency and that the picture is indeed no more than a colour photocopy.

The images are then pretty much disposable. It is not the end of the world if they are never returned and they make a huge visual impact if they are sent as part of the presentation.

If I have an article that will really benefit from the inclusion of the photos, I insert these laser prints between the loose leaves of the manuscript.

A front cover followed by a big bold picture, followed by good text, interspersed with further pictures, looks very good. I really believe that this sort of presentation helps to sell a piece of work.

All you need to know about image orientation.

Photographs are oblong, not square. The image can therefore be wide and short or tall and narrow. There is one universally correct way to describe the orientation: landscape or portrait. It is easy to remember if you think about the subject matter that these two words relate to.

A portrait of a person tends to be taller than it is wide, whereas a picture of a landscape tends to be wider than it is tall.

Portrait

A front cover or a full page of a magazine is suited to p o r t r a i t photographs.

Landscape

When you start splitting a page up there is scope for both. Half a page is ideal for a landscape whereas a quarter page suites a portrait better.

Chapter 8

Getting known, getting published

Reputation counts for a great deal in any walk of life. The need to get known as a travel writer and photographer is an important part of building up your business. The more you get published the more you get known, and the more you get known the more you get published. It is human nature to give work to people that you know.

Credits and the by-lines

The very first time you get something published you get a great feeling. Seeing your work in print appeals to the vainer sides of your character and gives you a buzz. The impulse is to ring all your friends and family and tell them about it, encouraging them to rush out and buy the newspaper or magazine with your published work.

Imagine how disheartening it is when they ring back and ask which piece was yours. It does occasionally happen that your name is left out by mistake, but you have a right to expect any of your work to be identifiable as yours.

Most photographs that are published will have a 'credit' printed next to them. This is a line that says who took the photo or who holds the copyright. It may be in very small print, but it does get noticed. Photographs that have been supplied to the publication by a photo library always seem to carry the name of the library but not always the name of the photographer as well. When both are shown the information is printed as 'Library/photographer' e.g. Travel Ink/Guy Marks at the side of the picture.

Quite apart from the ego trip of seeing your name in print, business contacts will notice that you have had something published. In fact I have had other people spot my name credited to photos that I didn't even know had been published. I was recently talking to the head of a PR company that has some very big clients in the travel business, including a tourist board. During the conversation it came out that she had seen my name credited to a picture in *marie claire* magazine. It was the first I knew of it, but she was right.

This just shows that people within the industry do take note of these credits, and it gives you the kudos and recognition that helps promote your business. I have also had people contact me after having seen a photograph of mine in a magazine. One particular photo of Ethiopia led to my being contacted by two quite separate tour companies, both of whom went on to buy photos from me for their forthcoming brochures.

If you haven't come across the expression 'by-line', it is just another word for a credit. It is usually associated with the written word rather than with photographs and is often in the introductory title to a piece. It stems from the phrase 'This piece is by...', hence a by-line. It is the writer's name and may or may not include further details about the individual or about the piece of writing.

The credit or the by-line is as good as an advertisement, and it's free. If you take out an advert saying 'I'm a writer' or 'I'm a photographer', editors and picture buyers are unlikely to read it. If you have a credit or a by-line, everybody can see that this really is what you do, and they can judge the quality of your work for themselves. Remember, too, that if your work is good enough to be published, it is good enough to stand up to those judgemental eyes.

Approaching new markets

When you are approaching a new market for the first time, these credits and by-lines become all-important. You always need to show people what work you have had published previously, and these credits are the proof. I often send in photocopies of articles that I have had published when I first contact an editor. I don't think for a moment that they have time to read right through all the cuttings, but they can see the length of the piece, the publication it was in and the all-important by-line and picture credits.

You need to try to sell yourself as much as you sell the actual writing and photography. It is no good making up things about your capabilities and your achievements because you will get found out and never get any more work. If you haven't yet had anything published, though, you should make a point of not mentioning it. Avoid the subject of previously published work and sell yourself on charm, knowledge and good looks. Yes, I know what you're thinking - that's why it's better to have something previously published!

It could be that the only work you have had published is in the local paper or even a village or club magazine. This doesn't matter at all. Getting published anywhere helps the cause. There is no shame in doing something for nothing either. Even if you don't get paid anything for your first pieces of work, or give the photos without charge, if you get into print you have crossed the first barrier. If your work is good enough to get into one publication it will certainly be good enough for others and perhaps next time you will get paid. At least you will get your name in print and have something to show to the next person you approach.

Once you get off the ground you can afford to take a different stance and divert your energies into the better-paying markets. Low-paid publications provide a great opportunity to get published initially, but you certainly don't owe them your undying gratitude for publishing your work. The commercial ones are making money from your input. When all you want is to get published that is fine, but once you have established your capabilities as a writer and photographer you will find that time becomes scarce and you simply cannot afford to spend your days working for nothing. Don't forget that you will have lots of non-earning days when you are out doing the actual travelling. Once back at your desk you will have to discipline yourself to do productive and financially viable work.

I can not emphasise enough, however, that getting anything published provides free publicity. If you want to have a successful business, you need credits and by-lines to build up your reputation. Do whatever it takes to get into print.

Networking

'Networking' is a word that I do not particularly like, but it has a rather explicit meaning. According to the dictionary it is 'the forming of business connections and contacts through informal social meetings'.

It is an extremely useful part of building up a business. All it means is getting yourself known by circulating in the right places. It is making yourself a part of an industry.

A chance meeting with someone may mean that they remember your name and what you do. When they see your by-line in a newspaper, a credit on a photo, or an article that you have written, their familiarity will become greater.

As soon as you become aware of something you see it everywhere. I'm sure that is somebody's law of nature but, if not, it should be - perhaps I can claim it for my own.

The effect of meeting someone on a social basis is to sensitise them to your existence. They may have never seen or heard of you before even though they have read some of the publications which you contribute to. Until the recognition is initiated, the eye will pass over your name without taking it in.

In actual fact most folk like to recognise someone just as much as the individuals like to be recognised. If you have just met someone in a social context and then you open a paper and see their name, you feel a certain affinity towards them. The name sinks in further and you become steadily more familiar.

'Networking' is making the most of this simple phenomenon. Being seen in the right places, or even in the wrong places, gets you known. If you can meet an editor, then there is far more chance that he will look at your proposal or article when it arrives on his desk, rather than be assigned to the massive piles of unknowns. Some even have a separate file for ideas that come in from people they know.

It is not just the editors that you need to get to know, it is the whole spectrum of people involved in the industry. This includes all the PR consultants that might be running press trips or at least might put you on their lists so that they can keep you up to date with their particular interests. Being well-informed is important and these guys actually want to tell you all about an aspect of the travel industry, and *that* is the industry you are trying to be a part of.

It's also good to get on friendly terms with the tour operators. If you ever come up with a commission that might be to their interest you will be able to approach someone that you know. They are far more likely to look favourably on requests for help with travel plans if they come from someone that is familiar to them. Help with travel plans could mean anything from taking a bit of time to give you some advice on where to go and how to get there, to actually offering you a free trip. Don't forget these guys are all specialists in their own particular field of operations and as a travel writer and photographer you need to be in touch with specialists. It is the quickest and easiest way to do research and to get accurate information.

Just the same as in any other social circle, meeting one person leads to being introduced to another. Little by little your network of contacts grows. A good place to meet people is at the travel shows that take place all around the country. Notably, there are shows in London, Bristol, Manchester and Edinburgh. The biggest is the *World Travel Market* at Earls Court, which takes place annually in November. Biggest is not necessarily the best, as it can be difficult to actually talk to anyone on anything but a very superficial level. I personally prefer the smaller exhibitions which have a much friendlier atmosphere, such as *The Independent Traveller's World* held in London and several other cities around the country. Then there is *Destinations* held at Olympia in London. New ones spring up every year; last year was the first year for a show called *The Daily Telegraph Adventure Travel and Sports Show* held in Chelsea Town Hall. This year the venue has changed to Olympia as well, but the point is that there are always exhibitions to go to. Most of them take place in January, February and March each year. The tour companies have stands and so do the tourist boards, airlines, travel book and magazine publishers. Even the newspapers tend to have a stand if they are sponsoring an event.

At many of the exhibitions there are talks and lectures given by people involved in the travel industry. Most are informative and interesting, but even in the unlikely event that you find a particular talk a little disappointing, at least you have been there, met people and been seen.

The same principle applies to travel clubs which have regular speakers talking about fascinating journeys that they've made. Just about any travel-related event is worth going to on the off-chance of renewing acquaintances and making new contacts. I met editors, writers and radio producers whilst attending as a member of the audience at a recording session of a radio travel programme. I've met publishers, authors and fellow freelance writers at book launches. I've met PRs, tour operators and marketing managers of tourist boards at the exhibitions and lectures.

This is networking, and this is something you can do which is pleasurable and costs very little, but as far as your business is concerned, it will be invaluable.

Chapter 9

Proposals and commissions

It is always very rewarding to write an article about your travels, send it into a newspaper or magazine, and get it accepted for publication. You write the piece because you want to, and simply send it in on spec. There is nothing stopping you doing this and certainly some of the articles I have had published have been sent in like this. Unfortunately it is not always a successful approach. There is no particular reason that the publication should want the article that you just happen to send in. They may have recently run a piece on a similar subject or have a similar one already in the pipeline.

This method does get results occasionally but it can be frustrating to write something and send it round to different editors, but never get it published. An unpublished article is a very sad thing; worthy but homeless through no fault of its own.

The alternative is to try to work more closely with the editors and write specifically for them. This doesn't mean that they will do the work for you and say 'I want an article about xyz, go away and write it'. The ideas for the articles invariably still have to come from you, the writer. This process of working together involves submitting proposals and then, if accepted, being commissioned to write the article and to take the photographs. This doesn't have to be dedicated to future travel plans. It can just as well arise from your previous travel experience. The main thing is that it is written to order rather than on spec. The commissioning editor is agreeing to take the article and to pay for it. Once that commitment has been made you are obliged to provide the article and the editor is obliged to pay for it, even if he decides not to publish it.

This does mean that editors are a little reluctant to commission articles, especially if they do not know you and your work. This obligation means that they are taking something on trust and agreeing to buy an article before it has even been written. They are taking a risk, and so the way you present your ideas has to be suitably appealing.

It quite often happens that an editor will say that he would be interested to see the finished piece. That way he is indicating an interest but will not actually commission you to write the piece. If he doesn't like it when he sees it he is not committed to taking it. If you are confident of your abilities, however, there is no reason why the article shouldn't be suitable. I take this sort of comment as a go-ahead and I write and submit the article. I've usually found that the editor is satisfied and accepts the piece. Without a fixed commission, however, you can't really approach people for help with your travel plans. There is a chance that the piece will never get published. Whether you get a commission or just an indication of interest in the idea, you still need to put your proposal to the editor in a suitable way.

I'm told that the biggest mistake people make in their approach to proposals is simply to tell the editor where they are going or where they have been. Phrases like 'I'm off to/just come back from Thailand - do you want an article about it?' are apparently absolutely the wrong thing to say. You will be told that Thailand is a destination not an article. It is the idea for the article that is needed, not simply a place name. That is fair comment in many cases and it is probably a very good rule of thumb to try not to take this approach.

I would say, though, that the ten commandments are the only rules I know of that are set in stone.

If you are ever able to get hold of a features list for a publication you will see how the editor's own approach somewhat contradicts this rule. Features lists give a list of forthcoming articles for the future issues. I've never yet seen one that is based around articles; rather, they are based on destinations. So it could be quite feasible to contact an editor to find out if they already have all the material they want for the particular destinations on their lists.

If you are just about to go to this destination or have just returned you may well be in with a chance of writing something for this planned features list. If the editor does say 'yes, we still have room' you then have to be quick off the mark. This is when you have to present your idea, and not be caught out by saying 'Oh I haven't actually got anything in mind, I was just wondering if you still needed material'. That will leave you looking very foolish indeed and you will not endear yourself to the editor. You are wasting his time unless you have an idea *before* you contact him. I still find myself doing this and I do occasionally get away with it, but it is a stupid and unprofessional way to go about things.

It is far better to put concrete proposals in front of an editor and see if he likes them.

Writing the proposal

The proposal could be quite detailed or just a few lines, depending on the subject matter and the circumstances. It is obviously quite difficult to give a clear idea about something you are intending to write if you haven't yet done the travel. The most interesting part of travel is the experience and the things that happen to you along the way. If it hasn't happened yet you can't know about it. The danger of over-stressing the content of the article is that it encourages you to look at your travels with pre-conceived ideas.

On the other hand you often need these pre-sold commissions to be able to get the travel facilities that you want. I mentioned this in chapter 2 where I looked at the ways to raise money and travel free.

What the actual proposal needs to include varies enormously. The best way I can illustrate this is to is to show three actual examples, all of which have resulted in commissions. The examples are very different in their approach. The first one is short but specific about its content and is based on previous travel. The second is based on a combination of telephone calls and written confirmations of finding an angle for a destination. The commission allows a trip to be made and enables me to get free travel. The third is based on a specialist travel subject, knowledge of which has been built up over several years. The proposal has to get this across and is an extremely detailed outline of a potential article. It even includes the first paragraphs of the article.

<u>Example 1.</u>

I noticed on a features list that an editor was intending to feature the broad topic of Africa. How vague can you get? For three issues in a row Africa was to be the subject. I spoke to the editor and she said one issue would be North Africa, one Central and East and the third would be Southern. I have travelled quite extensively in Africa and felt sure I could write something that would suit at least one of the issues. This is a huge section of the world and it would have taken forever to write detailed proposals on a topic for every country I've been to.

I wrote eight proposals that were no more than ideas. Each was based on an experience in a different country but transformed the destination into the bones of an article. Each proposal or idea was only a paragraph long.

This is what I wrote for Zimbabwe:

Zimbabwe:

- Victoria Falls: - This is perhaps Africa's most visited tourist site. As if the Falls themselves weren't enough, a number of activities have grown up around them. People now need several days to visit the area to take in some white-water rafting or canoeing on the Zambezi, a sunset booze cruise, horse-back safaris, flights over the Falls in planes, helicopters and microlights, and even bungey jumping from the bridges.

The editor rang me quite late one night and asked for this piece on Victoria Falls. She wanted about 1000 words, and the deadline was only about a week. Obviously with such a short time span this could only be written from previous travel experience. There would not have been time to organise a trip to the Falls, as well as time to travel around, come back and write the article. I knew that this was the way that this particular magazine worked so I only offered pieces that I could actually write from previous experience, but it is important to establish that this is the case when you are submitting a proposal. It would be useless if you got the commission and couldn't write the article because you hadn't been there.

I'm pleased to say the article was published and I was able to supply photographs to accompany the piece.

Proposals and commissions

<u>Example 2.</u>

I had been discussing the possibility of going to Finland both with the Finnish Tourist Board and with a magazine editor. This perhaps contradicts my earlier comments about article ideas rather than destination names. It is the way in which it was done, however, that is important. It is quite different to sound something out when you happen to be talking to someone anyway, than to ring them up specifically and exclusively to ask about a destination with no article in mind. The editor indicated that she might potentially be interested in the destination if I could find a suitable angle for an article. I researched the possibilities a little further. I needed to find out what sort of thing I could do in Finland and decide how I could tailor an article to that particular magazine.

After a couple of conversations we agreed in principle. My proposal was very brief and read:

"To re-cap - I propose looking at the Saimaa Lakeland area of the country. This is Europe's largest inland waterway and is an area of outstanding beauty - lakes dotted with forested islands. A number of activities commonly take place around the lakes in the summer such as trekking, boating of various kinds, cycling, fishing etc. I would hope to get an overview of a number of these activities on the trip. I don't want to tackle this article with too precise a preconceived structure, as the trip itself will determine what I write."

The commissioning letter I received was equally suitably vague and read:

<u>Length</u> 2000 words

<u>Commission details</u>
An anecdotal look at the Saimaa Lakeland area of Finland.

A factpage to also be supplied - exact length and scope tbc post trip.

<u>Photographs</u>
Will be considered

Well, this was sufficient to get things started. I'm off to Finland with a specific commission to write and it will be published. I don't have a confirmed publication date yet but I would imagine it will be out before this book is. This is the sort of commission that has allowed me to get a tourist board to help with my travel plans. The article is pre-arranged, sold before it is written, but not pre-conceived in its exact content. It has stemmed from the idea of the destination rather that the piece itself, but has been tailored to suit the requirements of a particular market. I am not tied to writing just one piece on Finland and have already put out feelers to see if anybody is looking for photographs of the area.

Example 3.

I knew that an editor was thinking of featuring the subject of overland travel. This is my speciality as I have done a considerable amount of overlanding. I also knew that several other writers would be putting in proposals on the subject so I had a lot of work to do to make my ideas sell over the competition.

Here I needed to have good ideas for the article but also to get across the point that this was my speciality and that I was the best person to write the material they required. The proposal is lengthy and took almost as long as writing an article in full. As I didn't know exactly what the magazine wanted I put in two alternative proposals.

Here are some extracts of the letter I wrote, and the proposals I enclosed:
"Dear... (editor),
I think you are familiar with the fact that my work has been published in a range of newspapers and magazines....

But what qualifies me to write about overlanding in particular?
Well this really is my speciality as I have been very involved with overlanding in all its different forms...

I followed on with details of my overlanding experience - almost like a CV. Then came the proposals themselves:

Proposals and commissions

Proposals for Overlanding article.

This is an extremely wide subject and there are various ways of dealing with it. For this reason I have made two different proposals. In my opinion both of these could work well but it is more a question of how much space you would want to devote to this subject.

Proposal 1.

An article of about 2000 words.

A short introduction will bring readers humorously into the first section of the article:
The discomforts of overlanding:

This section allows the Wilbur Smith quote to be introduced; "*Holiday from Hell*" (exact quote to be checked). The discomforts are often the funniest parts of a trip which should hold the readers' attention. The main issues in the section are:

- The basics - Lack of toilet and washing facilities, limited water.

- No beds for months - Low budget hotels - if at all, some of the worlds' worst accommodation.

- Cooking - Limited supplies - perhaps for a large group. Some dreadful meals of vegetable slop. Overuse of dehydes.

- Dealing with the elements - camping, the vehicle and the elements, getting stuck in mud...

- Vehicle reliability - breaking down and repairing the vehicle if this is your responsibility.

The next section of the article redresses the balance with these downsides and gives some reasons why people go overlanding despite these discomforts.

The pleasures of overlanding

- Accessibility - Getting to places where there is no public transport, off the beaten track. An itinerary planned around what is best to see rather than where you can easily get to.

- Freedom & Independence - Self contained and self sufficient for long periods and distances so can camp in the middle of a desert or rain forest.
Sleeping out under the stars. e.g. -watching the dawn break over the Amazon while all the passengers were still asleep in their hammocks, swinging from the trees.

- Seeing the world from ground level - not from the top floor of a 5 star hotel mixing with locals as you buy food from their local markets. Stopping in small villages that are not "tourist destinations".

- Slow pace of trips - usually gives time to stand and stare - see how the ordinary folk of a country live.

- An eye-opener - to third world lives. Gives an education in the basics of life. Makes us appreciate the good things of our own society but question priorities.

The next section will deal with the social aspect of overlanding, the people you travel with rather than the people and places you have gone to see.

Travelling with others.

- Friendships - Can be made or can be strained.

- Tolerance - (and lack of) in large groups.
Learn a great deal about other people especially that we all see things differently. Often learn a lot about yourself; shortcomings and strengths.

- <u>Travelling with like minded people</u> - someone to share the experiences with. Need to talk to people from your own society/ culture.

- <u>People leave their brains at home when they go on holiday</u> - quotes from pax: "If I ring home from Nairobi will my mother be in?"
Whilst travelling through Brazil - "Is that the Nile?"

- <u>Daft things that passengers do</u> - Jeopardising others' safety by buying firearms in Pakistan a few days before we are about to cross into Iran just after the Gulf War.
One woman stopped taking her medication because it made her pee and didn't want to have to keep stopping the truck - without medication her leg swelled up and she got gangrene and had to be abandoned at the next hospital.

<u>End the article</u> on a high note tying in the points that if you can't see the funny side of things or cope with the discomforts then you shouldn't go on this sort of trip; indeed it *isn't* a "holiday". If you can cope, then, despite these daft incidents, much of the trip will be amusing, fun, educational, adventurous, exciting and an experience of a lifetime.

Here are the **first couple of paragraphs** as an example for the article:

"Boys at the front girls at the back". When toilets don't exist and the only cover for miles is your vehicle itself, then this kind of *on the road* etiquette maintains some sort of decorum. It takes some getting used to but after a while the base lines of normality are lowered and even the taboos of bodily functions and digestive disorders become topical conversations around campfire mealtimes. On long overland trips there are days when things look so bleak that it seems the bottom has fallen out your world, but these are nothing compared with the days when the world falls out of your bottom.

Overlanders always get plenty of advice about what to take on a trip, such as loo paper, medicine, and a sense of humour. Occasionally though, these things just aren't enough and I would suggest you include a few extras in your kit such as; a spare fuse - for when yours blows, a couple of marbles - because you're bound to meet someone who's missing some, a screwdriver for that inevitable loose screw, and most important of all, a spare rag - because you *will* lose yours...

Proposal 2.

Although the ideas of proposal 1 are workable, there is a great deal to fit into a single article and by necessity a great deal thus has to be left out.

If space were available to do **a two part article split over two issues** then far more subjects could be included.

Within this two part article I would be able to cover the issues underlined in the notes below, incorporating the points from proposal 1 at the appropriate places.

The piece would be divided into what I consider to be two very distinctly different topics.

These are:

Part 1.
An article of about 2000 words.
Going it alone - overlanding with your own vehicle.

Proposals and commissions

●   <u>Long journeys overland</u> - What is overlanding; shorter trips with own vehicle tend to be trial runs for bigger plans.

●   <u>What you need</u> - Vehicle, tools, spares, guts

●   <u>Adventure</u> - Danger, foolhardiness. Be prepared

●   <u>Where to go</u> - Having decided the route. The need to find out what there is to see and do along the route.

●   <u>Alone or not</u> - with a partner, small group, or friend/ travelling companions? Travelling in convoy.

●   <u>Cost</u> - comparative cost against public transport and commercial tours.

Part 2.
An article of about 2000 words.
Overlanding with a tour company

●   <u>Long or short journey</u> - Time available, where you want to go. Should perhaps do a short overland to start with to see if it is your sort of thing.

●   <u>Overland or safari</u> - glorified or rather undersold - are your expectations the same as the product that is on offer.

●   <u>Why go with a tour company?</u> - The drawbacks but the ease of arrangement.

●   <u>The problems of travelling with a group.</u>

●   <u>The companies</u> - value for money?

End

Well that was a tremendous amount of work, but it paid off. I got the commission. The commissioning letter came confirming that they wanted an article of 2500 words about 'A look at overlanding, primarily the organised variety, as in your Proposal #1'.

Having put all the work into the proposal the article itself was relatively easy to write. Using my own proposal as a guide, I was able to work out how long each part of the article should be in order to include all the points that I had mentioned. It worked out well and the whole thing was published along with 5 photographs. I assure you, 2500 words and 5 photographs makes the work worthwhile.

What is more I have since been commissioned to write the second part of the proposal - another article of 2400 words on self-drive overlanding.

Photographic commissions

Photographic commissions have to be considered in a number of different ways. Obviously the articles that I have just discussed also included photographs and so to an extent the photographs are proposed along with the words. The phrase "photographs will be considered" on the commissioning letters shows that they are seen as a separate issue by the editors.

They will not commit themselves in advance to taking any photographs. They want to actually see the photos first and only then will they decide how many they will use, if any at all. Of course if you know your market and take suitable photos the chances are that some will be taken with the articles, but they are not pre-sold by commission.

Some publications run photo features and if you are proposing this sort of piece, you need to treat it in the same way as the proposals for articles. You need to put the ideas across and probably need to send samples of the photographs you have in mind. Until you become well known you are very unlikely to get a fixed commission for a photo-led article prior to travel, but after you have a proven track record there is no reason why this type of proposal should not be just as acceptable to editors.

If you already have travel plans arranged it is much easier to approach people with ideas. Contacting libraries, publishers and picture researchers and letting them know where you are going could well lead to getting the right photos that will sell on your return. I mentioned in passing to a guide book publisher that I'm going to Mexico later in the year. It just happens that they are bringing out a guide to Mexico and haven't yet got the cover shot. I have been told exactly the requirements and should be able to come up with the right shot. This is not exactly a commission as there is no commitment or obligation involved. It does amount to a proposal and an intention, however, and had I not pre-arranged this, there would be little chance of coming back with a suitable photo for this market.

I've been fortunate enough to get a number of photographic commissions from tour operators who need photographs for their brochures and promotions. I have mentioned this in some detail in the section on paid commissions in chapter 2. The only way to get these commissions is to make yourself known to the tour operators. You have to be competitive and you are up against any number of people who will go and do this in return for a free trip. It is essential to be able to show that you can deliver not just a quantity of photographs, but a number of *useable* photographs. These companies often have specific requirements and you have to be able to take the shots that they want rather than the shots that you want.

You might think that these commissions are more for the professional photographer than the travel writer and photographer. My attitude is that I hope to be as professional in my photography as I am in my writing and that is really the theme of this book. This is how you make the whole thing pay; do both and be prepared to be professional at both. You can just as easily fine-tune your photographic skills as you can your literary skills.

Chapter 10

The mechanics of a travel article

I am quite sure that every travel article that has been written has some point of interest to it, or the writer would not even have considered the subject matter. Transforming that subject into a readable and saleable piece is the all-important skill.

It only takes a matter of minutes to read an article and it seems to me that the best ones read as though they only took a few minutes to write. I like the impression of a one-to-one narrative, as though I'm face to face with the writer and he is actually there, telling me the story in those few minutes it takes to read the words.

To get this impression from a piece of written work takes anything but a few minutes. It is a matter of technique and structure, as well as individual style, that makes the piece come across well. You need to be able to make an article flow smoothly and you need to hold the readers' attention.

You never see a guide to writing telling you that your work needs an end, a middle and a beginning. They put it the other way round and lose your attention. Your mind thinks that the writer is stating the obvious and skips on to the next thing of interest.

The importance of the three parts to an article is absolutely fundamental to success and you really need to appreciate what is meant by those three basic words that are used to describe the sections.

The first paragraph sells the article. Editors do not usually have time to read right through a piece to find out if they like it. They can tell from the first paragraph or two whether or not they are interested. It may seem very harsh and is a bit like judging a book by its cover, but unfortunately that is the way things are. It's not just the editors that do it, we all do. I never read a newspaper or a magazine from cover to cover. We all flip through publications, glance at the headline, the title and then the first couple of paragraphs to decide if we want to read on. If the subject doesn't grab us by then we cruelly dismiss it and move on to another piece.

If you do carry on reading then there is a natural expectation for the bulk of the article to be as interesting as the initial impression. It should expand on the theme that was set in this first scene and this middle section is where the story is told.

Ultimately the story has to be brought to an end. If it just stops it can seem far too abrupt. The reader feels cheated. They feel that they have wasted their time reading all the way through an article to find out what happens and then, all of a sudden, nothing happens. It's like a joke without a punch line. It aggravates people. This doesn't have to be some earth-shattering conclusion, a moral or profound statement, it just has to be rounded off. It is surprising how a few carefully chosen words will bring something to a tidy close and satisfy the reader.

Case study

The best way I can illustrate these points is to relate them to an actual piece of writing. I've decided to use one of my own published articles as a case study because I know the process I went through to write it and get it published. It is not perfect by any means but I can happily criticise it without offending anyone but myself and can be satisfied in the knowledge that it was published in the prestigious travel pages of the Financial Times.

The sound of nervous laughter still pealed through the night air long after the rumble and the explosion from the crater had subsided. Scattered lumps of fallen larva glowed on the ashen slopes and faded into their surroundings.

The laughter waned to a hush as we waited for the next eruption. Another pyrotechnic explosion lit the sky, as red hot molten larva was coughed high into the air from the mountain's throat. For a split second the sky was alight but silent.

Sound followed light. Our uncontrolled physical reactions welled within. Smiles broke on faces with pleasure and sheer wonderment. Then the adrenaline of angst and the fear of foolhardiness forced laughter from our gaping mouths.

The molten missiles reached their zenith and turned. They hurtled to the ground with all the splendour of a Guy Fawkes display. Unlike fireworks, however, they didn't burn themselves out in mid-air, but landed with a thud, a semi-solid splat, expanding and efflorescing as they cooled.

I knew I shouldn't be here. I had been staying in Antigua, and could easily have spent the day shopping in the Indian market or simply sitting under the jacaranda in the main square admiring the colonial architecture. But for some inexplicable reason I had forsaken the safety and comfort of a hotel room and had, along with my companions, signed up for a half day's trip to the active volcano Pacaya.

It was 1987 since its last major eruption so I was expecting little more than a smouldering hill or a bubbling crater, even though Pacaya had a reputation of being Guatemala's most spectacular volcano. Yet, there I was, staring the very forces of nature in the face, with plumes of larva jetting from the mountain. We were pushing our luck to the limits, and our excitement to new thresholds.

What I thought was to be only an hour's walk had turned into a three hour uphill struggle. The pack of cameras on my back had become heavier with every step, but it was a beautiful wooded hillside on which to be spending an afternoon, and there was the promise of a spectacular view of the volcano when we reached the top.

We could hear the distant rumbles becoming louder and nearer, and every now and then there was a gap in the trees and a glimpse of the summit beyond us. Tired, we stopped at the ridge. It was late afternoon and at last we had a clear view of the volcano. This, I thought, would be as close as we would get. Every now and then there was a deep rumble and a cloud of smoke belched up from the cone. The smoke was thick and dark but in the daylight I couldn't tell that it concealed bursts of hot larva.

At the edge of the wood the vegetation gave way to a black larva field, a kind of dusty gravelly incline. At a high point I could see a concrete block, presumably a marker and the limit of accessibility. As I got closer, however, one of my companions pointed to some distant specks way up on the volcanic cone itself. Yes; people were actually trekking up the side of an active volcano, and it looked impossibly steep.

"It will take about another hour from here," said our guide, "the going gets difficult. It is very steep and there is a lot of loose ground. Some of you can stay here if you like and we will collect you on the way down. We must hurry because it will soon be dark. It is a very difficult climb. Stay here if you can't make it."

I understood what he was saying, but really didn't appreciate how difficult the climb would be, or just why he was so keen not to be stuck halfway up the cone with anyone who couldn't move quickly. I was already tired and didn't relish the prospect of another hour's climb. Having come this far, however, it seemed foolish not to continue, and I forged on.

"Loose ground" was an understatement. There was a route that others had taken, crushing the brittle pumice that slipped from underfoot.

I was happy to take two paces forwards and one back. I would have crawled on all fours but for the fact that the pumice would have removed the skin from my hands.

The peak of the volcano split into twin cones. One that was erupting while we climbed the steep slopes of the other. As we got closer and the light started to fade, I realised that there were pieces of molten larva spewing forth with every smoky eruption. These molten rocks were falling on the side of the cone to produce the ashy larva field.

There was, however, no distinction between the larva field on the one cone from the larva field on which we climbed. It was one continuous bed of rock and ash, down one slope and up another. As we got closer the eruptions became more vigorous and the larva started to fall across our intended path.

"Go left! Go left" shouted our guide. We didn't need to be told twice.

I clambered away from the path, heading to my left and ever upwards. The rocks were jagged and unsteady, and fell away in landslides as I tried to pick out a route. My hands went out in front of me to steady my ascent and, to my horror, the ground was warm; with wisps of steam sneaking out between small fissures.

The excitement, or perhaps it was the fear, gave me a new spurt of energy. I scrambled over the rocks and arrived gasping for breath at the summit just as the sun sank below the horizon to one side of the smouldering crater.

The eruptions came thick and fast. Each new explosion seemed to come with more force and the fall-out spread wider. One piece landed a matter of yards from where we were standing. It had looked so small way up in the sky, just like the falling remains from a firework, but in the last split seconds as it loomed towards the ground I realised that these were huge boulders, not insignificant little rocks. A few people - not part of our party - ran down to examine the fallen rock.

Amazed that their guide hadn't stopped them, our own guide decided that this was the time to warn us of the dangers.

He seemed to know the limits. He watched each ensuing eruption, as though he could tell exactly where things would fall by how high and how vigorously they had been expelled from the earth. But he admitted that many people had been caught out. People had died up there. The explosions had been known suddenly to come out of the side of the mountain and catch people unawares, rather than out of the crater mouth. I wondered what was stopping the smouldering ground on which I stood from opening up, from melting into the magma.

I put my trust in the guide; not because of his reputation or ability, but simply because I had no choice. When he finally said it was time to go, I believed him.

Chronologically this article is about staying in Antigua, deciding to take a half day excursion, walking up a wooded hillside, walking up a volcanic cone, watching the eruptions and leaving again. But that is not the order in which I have structured the piece.

The most exciting part of the story is the erupting volcano, so that is where I have started.

The first paragraph goes straight in with '*nervous laughter*', a little anticipation and an explosion.

This is intended to capture the reader's interest and to set the scene. It summarises the article in that it tells you immediately that this piece is about watching an erupting volcano. The editor to whom it was submitted can instantly decide if he is not interested in the subject. If he is, he can read on.

The bulk of the article is the 'middle' section. Here the whole story is told. The piece goes back to the chronological beginning and explains how I came to be at the top of that volcano. It is put into geographical context, mentioning the town of Antigua and the country - Guatemala. I have often read articles that assume the reader knows every obscure place in the world which I think is a bit of an elitist attitude; it means that you are only writing for people who already know the area. I like to put in the geographical location reasonably early on in the piece, although if you put it in the first paragraph it may detract from what you are trying to do with those opening lines.

This middle section is the place to get lots of information across. It is often helpful to build the article around such subjects as history, local people, what a place is like in terms of accommodation, safety and even features like strikingly beautiful plants.

If you look back at the article you will see in this particular case I have included many of these topics. I mention history when I say '*1987 since its last major eruption*'. By mentioning colonial architecture it suggests a longer line of historical interest and also gives an idea of the physical appearance of the buildings. Local people are mentioned with the words '*Indian market*' and this also helps create atmosphere and gives information of what there is to do. Shopping is always a good thing to mention - most people like to know there is something to buy that is typical of the area. '*Safety and comfort of a hotel room*' actually says quite a lot about the place; it conveys the fact that there are hotels and also the all-important ingredients for all travellers - safety and comfort. The other thing I mention is the jacaranda tree. I must admit I don't describe it so I am myself being elitist by assuming people know what it is. Having said that you can't describe in detail every single thing that takes your interest or the article will never end. The point is that those familiar with the magnificent lilac-mauve blossom on the jacaranda will be able to picture the scene in some detail.

These are all key points that perhaps tell you far more about the place that you first realise through a casual glance at the piece. Most of these points don't even relate to the actual volcano, but they give a wider picture and set a foundation for the main trek.

Still within the middle section, I carry on to the actual subject of the trek. There is a great deal of description of what it was actually like. I mention the time of day and how long it all took, distance and views, discomfort and elation, the vegetation, the rocks and the ground underfoot. The whole thing is brought to a climax by reaching the top of the volcano and seeing the eruptions. This brings us back to the opening comments. We started with the climax and then the bulk of the article takes you through the paces to actually get to that climax. Each paragraph is linked to the previous one in such a way that the story flows. It becomes difficult for the reader to stop reading; he wants to know what happens next and is led into it.

The next thing to consider is how to end the article. Really there is not much to say once you have brought the reader to the top of the volcano and shown them the pyrotechnics, but I can't just leave the reader up there. I needed a device to get them down and round it off. I didn't want to describe the descent and cover the same ground again so the descent had to be implied rather than actually taking place.

This end piece only needs to be a paragraph or even a short sentence but it is an important part of the structure of an article. I like to think the one in the example worked.

Why it sold

I am convinced that a deciding factor in the saleability of this article was the photographs. Let's face it, they are spectacular. The piece was published with two photographs. I've used one of them on the cover of this book, so that you can see for yourself, one of the series of the volcano erupting. The other was a very large photo of a street in Antigua that is dominated by a volcano in the background. The fact that the volcano in the background of Antigua is not actually the same one that was erupting is of little importance and, I might add, was a point that was missed by whoever wrote the captions at the newspaper.

So the visual impact attracted the attention of the editors. I know this for a fact because one editor rejected the piece with these words "...I am afraid that I don't feel the piece is right for us (the first page is over-written); and, sadly, your excellent photographs need colour to have impact, and we only have black-and-white newsprint..."

I took this as a very positive sign even though it was a rejection. It is quite unusual for an editor to take the time to tell you why they have rejected a piece and this can certainly be seen as an encouragement. It was practical criticism which allowed me to look again and improve the piece. I could quite see what the editor meant, this piece was indeed over-written. I guess over-written meant an excessive use of flowery language with just too many adjectives so that the whole thing was a little bit over the top. I toned the whole thing down considerably from my original submission although quite possibly not enough. His point about colour newsprint was something over which I had no control, but most papers have the ability to print colour when the budget is allocated to the travel pages.

It is also worth remembering that different papers print different styles and this particular piece wasn't right for that publication. I hadn't done my market research, I'd just sent it in to anybody on spec.

I re-wrote, thought again about the market and submitted it to a different newspaper where this type of article was more suitable. This time it worked. The piece was accepted. I still think it was a little over-written, but there was sufficient of worth in it, along with the photos, for the editor to accept it. Getting accepted is the single essential part of making it pay.

The editor obviously also thought it was slightly over-written but was prepared to take the time to improve it. Editors will only do this if they think the time spent on an article will be worthwhile. They can't really re-write the whole piece, but they can edit it.

There were quite a few editorial changes from my original submission to what you see printed here. Phrases like '..time honoured laws of nature..' were removed. I had referred to Antigua as a 'picturesque little town'. This too was cut; frankly I agree - it says nothing about the place and uses an unnecessary travel cliché. Another sentence laboured the point about the ground being difficult to make progress across - this never made the newsprint. So lots of relatively small changes made the finished piece more readable. Despite these changes, I am sure it would not have sold had it not been for the basic structure, content, style and visual impact.

Simien Mountains, Ethiopia - page 178

Djemaa el Fna, Marrakesh, Morocco - page 179

The Golden Temple of Amritsar, Punjab, India - page 179

Portraits - page 179

Chapter 11

Portrait of a photograph

This chapter deals with the aesthetics and construction of photographs in a similar way that the previous chapter deals with the mechanics of an article. There are rules, guidelines and techniques in photography that help make a good picture. Rather than list these features of composition I have chosen to give the information by example. Each of the photographs in this book has been included to make some particular point. Taken together, the comments made about the various images give a considerable amount of what I hope will be useful information and tips on the subject.

Pacaya Volcano, Guatemala
front cover

This photograph of an erupting volcano in Guatemala was taken from the top of the twin peak of the volcano. You may think it has been taken from some distance with a high magnification telephoto lens, but that was not the case. I was so close to the subject that pieces of larva were actually falling behind me having shot overhead. You can read about this experience, as I use an article about it as a case study in chapter 10.

The picture was taken with a Pentax ME Super and a Vivitar 19mm manual lens. The film was Fujichrome Sensia 400 ISO. A tripod and cable release were used.

This was quite an extraordinary subject to try to photograph. The scene in the night sky was so big that I needed this ultra wide-angle lens to fit all of the erupting larva into the frame. There was not a great deal

161

of light compared with a daylight scene, so to capture the available light I needed a fast film, a large aperture and also a long exposure time (slow shutter speed).

There is absolutely no way you could hold a camera steady enough for such a long exposure so I had to use a tripod. The shutter was released with a cable so that I didn't even have to touch the camera, which would have risked shaking it and blurring the image.

I used the camera's internal light meter to decide on the correct exposure. By setting it on automatic I could see what the camera thought the exposure should be as I held it up and pointed it to the centre of each explosive eruption. As night came on and the overall light diminished the exposures went off the end of the automatic scale. This is when informed guesswork comes into determining the exposure.

I set the camera to 'B'. This setting means 'bulb' and has the effect of keeping the shutter open for as long as you keep the release button depressed. I could activate the cable, count to four or five, and then close the shutter again. I say four or five because I took several different shots, determined to get at least one good one. By doing this I produced a whole series of shots at different exposures each with a different effect. The shorter exposures freeze the action so you can pin-point the individual pieces of larva. The longer exposures give the effect of trails of light following the trajectory of the glowing molten rock.

I think this shows that good photos can be taken with relatively inexpensive equipment; chapter 5 on tools of the trade elaborates on this. A fast film like this has large grain and doesn't have the colour accuracy and saturation depth that I normally want. With slower films, however, the exposure time would have been so excessive to get an image that the eruptions would have come and gone before the picture was created. I don't carry much fast film, but this just shows that it is worth having a roll or two for the unexpected opportunity.

Pigs in Paradise, Honduras
page 49

This photograph was taken on the Caribbean coast of Honduras at a village called Sambo Creek.

I have included this shot for its content rather than for any technical details about the equipment and exposures.

A common image of the basic ingredients for a paradise are a long white sandy beach with palm trees, coconuts and some fresh water nearby. Sambo Creek was just such a place and this is just one of the many photos I took there.

As soon as I saw this particular scene I thought to myself 'even the pigs are in paradise'. The title of an article immediately flashed through my mind like a newspaper headline - Pigs in Paradise at Sambo Creek.

It is strange how seeing something through a camera lens can give you an instant idea. The photo and the title came hand in hand - all I had to do then was write the article.

I did get around to writing it and two different versions of it have already been published, one of which included this photo and carried the title 'Pigs in Paradise'. It just shows that a photo not only sells the article but can actually inspire you to write the article in the first place.

There are a few points about the composition of the photo that might interest you.

You can see from the foreground that I have had to walk into the water to take the shot from a suitable angle. If I'd taken the picture from the shore it would just have looked like pigs in any old bit of water so it is very important to take some trouble to position yourself correctly.

The pig nearest to me is positioned in such a way that its snout points to the bottom left hand corner of the frame and its bottom upwards and inwards towards the centre of the picture; this creates a diagonal line along the pig's back that draws the eye into the scene.

The next two lines that the eye comes to are the shore and the top of the boat. These are not horizontal but at an angle so they do not cut the picture in half. They mirror each other around the horizontal with one sloping downwards and the other upwards. Downward lines are depressing and upward lines are happy, so this gives balance. The happy line is made dominant because it has a more striking colour and the depressing line is softened by being broken by the shapes of the pigs' backs.

Next we come to the centre of the picture. There is a man in the shadows sitting under a palm tree. It looks like he is just whittling away at a piece of wood - this little scene within a scene adds human interest and reaffirms that image of paradise. Then there is a bit of grass and some huts. The harshness of their lines is broken by the palm tree trunks in front of them. They add a bit of colour which just lifts the eye out of the predominant greenness and creates some visual interest. One of the huts is thatched with palm fronds which lends some atmosphere to counter the shed-like structure of the pink block.

The palm trees give a nice frame to the picture, filling in the top corners with some mid-ground interest. The background serves its purpose - it is something against which to view the scene. It is a jungle-covered hill with steamy mist rising from it. The cloud effect that this causes is in subtle contrast to the bright sunshine that lights the foreground and gives defined shadows to the middle ground.

In brief this is just a pleasing image that gave me an idea for a very profitable article. With further analysis, though, you can see how a considered approach to the content of a picture produces that pleasing image. If you can make the picture work so that it inspires you to write then you are well on the way to making it pay.

Tanks and Travellers, Eritrea
page 50

These two photographs were taken in Eritrea and are, in fact, of the same tank. By taking the photograph from a different angle and with different inclusions two very different pictures have been produced. Making full use of the scene has provided me with pictures aimed at a number of unrelated markets.

The picture with the travellers peering into the wreckage is very much a tourism picture. It shows clearly that despite being a piece of war debris, it is in an area accessible to travellers. I used it to illustrate an article about the re-birth of tourism in Eritrea.

The second picture, taken just by asking my travelling companions to stay out of shot, has a very different feel to it. It is far more suitable for use in an article about the past armed struggle in the country and is more of a war picture than a tourism picture. This photograph is ideal as a stock shot for a library. It is non-specific and could therefore have many applications. There is nothing that distinguishes it or limits it to being specific to Eritrea. There are no people that limit use, nor is there anything that is going to date the picture and reduce its useful life (except for the inevitable progress of the design of the instruments of war).

The photos were taken whilst I was carrying out a commission for a tour operator. I provided them with several photographs taken at this old battle scene, but also kept these ones for my own use. Both of these photographs have been published and the sales have helped make the initial commission more profitable.

Local Transport, Eritrea
page 50

The local transport says an awful lot about a country. Do they have fast cars and high speed railways or donkeys, carts, buses, boats or rickshaws? It is a subject that often puts a country in perspective and could pictorially add a dimension to an article, covering a subject that didn't make it into the text. In fact this is just the way in which this picture of a Bedford 'bus' was used in an article I wrote about the country.

You may think that the composition of this shot is rather odd; there is a lot of dead area of blue sky and similarly dead area of foreground, with the subject right in the middle. It doesn't exactly fill the frame which is what you are usually told to do.

The point of this type of framing is to aim for a front cover. Whether it is for a book, a brochure, or a magazine there is room to put the title and descriptive text over this dead space without spoiling the composition of the picture. If it is not going to be used in this way, the top and bottom can always be cropped. It is far more difficult to add to a picture than to crop it.

Pushkar Camel Fair, Rajasthan, India
page 51

This photograph was taken when the sun was just going down which gives that very special warm light that glows around reddish brown colours. Sand and camels are ideal subjects for this time of day.

The picture was taken with a Pentax ME Super, with a 28mm Tamron manual lens. The film was Fujichrome 50 ISO.

My companion wandered away saying "you're not taking more photos are you? - the light has almost gone". The light was changing with every minute and I think this justified taking photographs until I could take no more. I didn't have a tripod with me so I had to use the largest aperture and fastest shutter speed that I could. That meant that any movement was frozen and, had I taken the tripod, it would have been tempting to go for a longer exposure and smaller aperture to maximise the depth of field. The results wouldn't have turned out as well, as it happens, because there would inevitably have been some blurred subjects from movement during the creation of the shot.

Again this shows that good photos can be achieved with the minimum of equipment.

So far this shot has been published about half a dozen times in brochures and magazines. I just about gave it away the first time, but it paid off. Having it in print gave me something to impress others with, and led directly to further sales.

Leaning tower of Pisa, Italy
page 51

This photograph is something of a travel cliché. Everyone who goes to Pisa takes photographs of each other holding up the tower. It is precisely because everybody does, that the picture has some pertinence to the site. Cliché or not, this photograph, which was taken whilst on commission, made the front cover of a travel brochure. People 'doing what tourists do' was exactly what the customer wanted.

I had very limited time when I went around this site - about twenty minutes to look all around and take all the shots I needed. I used my

Nikon F4S and the wide-angle end of the scale of my 35-70mm autofocus lens. This lens gave me the scope to have a good depth of field with both the foreground and background adequately in focus. The matrix light metering of this camera allowed me to snap away without having to think too much about exposure settings.

All you need to know about models

When is a model not a model? When they're an incidental.

If you take a picture of a crowded market scene, the people in the market are incidental. They have not been asked to model for the photograph and they are not in themselves essential to the photograph; it could have been anybody passing, not a specific individual.

If, on the other hand, you ask someone to pose for a photograph or they are the main subject of that photograph, they are in effect modelling for you.

If you intend to publish the photograph you need their permission. If you are going to sell the picture for advertising purposes the customer will normally insist that there is a written release form available in which the model has given their permission.

This permission does not have to be based on a financial payment. Subjects are often delighted at the prospect of appearing in a published photograph, but if they have posed, their permission must be sought.

It is a little bit of a grey area in that if a person has agreed to pose for you it suggests they are willing for their picture to be used. This permission is therefore often implied but if you don't actually have that in writing, certain markets will not consider your work.

Agreements with slide libraries often specify that you must have model release forms available for all work submitted unless you have told them to the contrary. The onus is on the photographer.

It is easy to draw up a simple agreement headed 'Model Release Form' which gives the photographer the rights to use the picture in any way he wants. Always carry some blank agreements in your camera bag.

Eiffel Tower at Night, Paris
page 51

This is another travel classic, one of the most identifiable landmarks of Paris. The Eiffel Tower must have been photographed from every angle and under all possible lighting conditions. Indeed there is nothing new about taking a shot of it at night from this viewpoint at the Palais de Chaillot. Just because it has been taken before, that doesn't mean that you can't take it again - taking a classic view is not like plagiarizing someone else's work. This is the sort of shot that gets used again and again, so if you are going to photograph Paris it is the sort of thing you want for your own personal library. I have had this particular photograph published in a travel brochure.

I've also included this shot to get across the point that all lighting conditions should be considered. It would be easy to spend a week in Paris and never actually get around to going out at night with a camera and tripod. Personally I think night shots of cities can be the most visually impressive views.

Spider Monkey, Costa Rica
page 52

This photograph of a spider monkey was taken in Costa Rica. It was taken with a Pentax ME Super, a Sigma 75-300 APO manual focus zoom lens, a tripod and cable release and the film used was Fujichrome Velvia 50 ISO.

It is not always possible to get the wildlife shots that you want. Wildlife specialists go to extreme lengths to get the fantastic shots that we have become accustomed to seeing. As a travel photographer rather than a wildlife photographer there is not usually the opportunity, equipment or time to spend day after day in jungles and rainforests tracking animals and making carefully constructed hides.

I did see lots of spider monkeys in Central American jungles. It was great to watch their characteristic movements as they swing through the canopy - their name seemed very apt. The chances of actually getting a useable shot from the ground, however, were remote. There is just too much vegetation in the way and you are in the dark, pointing your camera upwards, with the light behind the subject.

By taking advantage of the local zoo, I was able to see one of these animals in full daylight. By watching them just for a few moments I was able to see which branch they liked to hang from and set up the camera in roughly the right position. Then I just had to wait, and made the final adjustments when the subject swung into frame. In this pose he shows all the characteristics that really say 'Spider Monkey'. The piece of bare stick is a bit of a giveaway as you would be unlikely to find that in a jungle situation, especially in such clear light.

By setting the aperture to the largest possible setting with a fast shutter speed I reduced the risk of the monkey's movement causing a blurred image. This setting also nicely throws the background out of focus which lets the eye concentrate on the monkey and not the bushes in the background.

There is nothing wrong with taking photos of captive animals as long as you do not sell them as shots of animals in the wild. Simply captioned 'Spider Monkey - Costa Rica' this shot doesn't claim to be anything more than it is. It has already been published five times.

Lalibela Priest, Ethiopia
page 85

This photograph was taken inside a rock-carved church in Lalibela, Ethiopia.

It was taken with a Samsung ECX1 compact camera. The film was Fujichrome Sensia 100 ISO.

I have included this photograph to show what excellent results can be achieved with a compact camera. I had not anticipated needing to take photographs inside the churches and so I didn't have my flash with me for my main SLR camera. Luckily I had the little Samsung in my bag.

The exposures were left up to the camera to decide, and were entirely automatic.

I am really extremely impressed that it has managed to give a depth of field that puts everything in focus from the writing in the bible to the murals in the background. I have avoided red-eye in this picture by taking it when the priest is not looking directly at me. I normally use a slower film, but the compact has a very slow lens which makes anything under about 100 ISO a bit impractical in daylight. The quality of this image is far better than I would have expected from a compact and I am more than happy with the colour saturation that has been obtained.

The image has already been published in two different publications.

Morning Glory Pool, Yellowstone National Park, Wyoming, U.S.A.
page 86

These two photographs illustrate the use of a polarising filter. They were taken within a few seconds of each other - just the time it takes to put a filter on the lens. In the first picture you can certainly see the pool, but there are lots of reflections on the surface of the water. There is glare from the sun and reflections of the clouds above and, if you look closely at the far edge of the pool, you can even make out a reflection of the distant tree-line. There is also steam rising from the subject, which doesn't help when you are trying to get a clear shot.

By fitting a circular polarizing filter I was able to cut out nearly all of the glare and reflection. You can see past the surface of the water right down into the earth to a strange channel from which this hot mineral-rich water emanates. This shot was taken only a few seconds later - you can see the clouds have moved slightly. You can also see that the filter cuts out some of the ambient light and gives the sky a much darker, richer blue colour.

These rich colour-saturated images are best captured on a film that does them justice. Fujichrome Velvia was used here to good effect.

Piazza di Spagna, Rome
page 86

This photograph was taken on a grey March day in Rome. I have used an ultra wide-angle lens, a Sigma 18-35mm. The scene is of the Fontana della Barcaccia with the Spanish Steps in the background.

This boat-shaped fountain is actually quite large as is the backdrop of the Spanish Steps. The ultra wide-angle has allowed me to get all of this into one shot.

Whilst it's true that the ultra wide-angle lens allows most of what you can see with your eyes to be included in the frame, its best use is not necessarily for taking in vast landscape scenes. Its most useful feature is its vast depth of field. It allows you to focus on both a large object in the foreground and distant objects in the background at the same time.

One thing you have to watch out for with these lenses is distortion. You tend to lose quality in the extremities of the picture, and straight lines can become curved. In this photograph you will see that the buildings on either side of the steps have been made to look as though they are leaning in towards the middle of the frame. This effect, known as converging verticals, can be something of a problem when you are photographing buildings.

If I had used a standard 50mm lens the buildings would have been vertical but I would only have had a small section of the fountain in shot. The converging verticals may not detract from the picture and can even be used to create an interesting picture when intentionally exaggerated. It is just a question of what effect you are trying to achieve.

White-water Rafting
page 87

This photograph was taken in the Tyrol region of Austria. It was taken with a Nikon F4S with a 75-300 autofocus zoom lens f/4.5 - 5.6. The film used was Fujichrome Velvia 50 ISO.

You have probably spotted that this photograph is not very sharply focused. There are lots of points to come out of this. I was using some very expensive equipment and what I consider to be a very good film. The result is far from perfect so it just shows that there is a bit more to photography than buying top-of-the-range kit.

This is an action shot that requires a very fast shutter speed to freeze the action. I was using a slow lens and wanted to finish off the last few shots of a slow film before I put in something more appropriate for the rest of the shoot. Because the raft was moving erratically and unpredictably through the water it wasn't practical to restrict the movement of the camera by fixing it to a tripod, so the camera was hand held.

This was a disastrous combination: a long slow lens, slow film, no tripod, and a fast-moving subject.

The lens was set to continuous autofocus and you can see from the clarity of the raft itself and the water that the camera was not at fault. The colours are good and at first glance this is an excellent photograph. The composition is good with the subject filling the frame, the people in the raft seem to be enjoying themselves, there is plenty of spray and the back of the raft is obscured by white water. It gives a great feeling of action. I offered this shot to the slide library I work with and was surprised when it was rejected. It was only then that I looked closely and realised that the people in the shot were blurred from movement. I contemplated throwing the image in the bin but decided I would keep it just because I liked the composition. I included it in a couple of submissions along with other photos that were much sharper.

To my delight this photo was published twice in the same week, once in full colour in a national broadsheet newspaper.

I think this shows quite a lot about technique and how mistakes can be made even with good equipment. It also shows that if the composition is good a photo will sell. Movement can add to a photograph, giving it some life and excitement. I could be cheeky and say that I intended to create this out-of-focus look to emphasise the sense of movement, but I didn't. In future, though, I will try to make a point of taking both sharp and blurred action shots so that editors can make their own choice about movement and its representation.

Black Bear, Alaska
page 87

This shot was taken with the same camera and lens as the white-water rafting shot, but this time I had a slightly faster film - Sensia 100 - and a tripod. The black bear is running upstream fishing for salmon. Bears literally chase the salmon around, confusing them until they are caught in shallows or stop because they don't know in which direction to swim to escape. The bear can then just pick them out of the water.

I used the tripod as a support, but did not have the ball-and-socket head fixed tightly, so that I could still move the camera to follow the movements of the bear. This wonderfully blurred shot which was the result is absolutely full of movement. The water is swirling in all directions and the slow shutter speed has added tracer lines to the splashes, though some of them are caught as clear water droplets. The bear is also moving which blurs his image, but the whole effect captures the spontaneity of the sudden, confusing movements.

Landscape Arch, Arches National Park, Utah, U.S.A.
page 88

The best time to take photographs is early in the morning or in the evening because the quality of light is completely different from normal middle-of-the-day lighting. When the sun is low in the sky there is an orange light that gives pictures a warm feeling. The effect is most noticeable on things like sandstone or anything which itself has an orange or ochre colour to it.

This picture of Landscape Arch was taken first thing in the morning, just as the sun was coming up. The light was changing by the second and in a series of photographs taken over a period of about five minutes each picture has its own characteristic light. Each change of colour only lasts a split second as the light changes with the angle of the rising sun.

As the effect lasts such a short time you have to do a certain amount of planning to get these shots. You need to spot what you think might make a good picture with this warm light well in advance. If you happen to see a great dawn or dusk shot by chance, there is every possibility that the opportunity will have passed by the time you get your camera set up. By their very nature, there is not a great deal of available light for these shots, so a tripod will be needed.

I noticed this arch whilst on a trek the day before and could see that the morning light would shine directly on the subject. I trekked out to the location again in the night so that by the time the sun came up, I was ready and waiting.

Colossus of Ramses II, Abu Simbel, Egypt
page 88

It is not always possible to be in the right place at the right time. I don't just mean for the chance shot, but for those dawn and dusk shots I mentioned above. Getting to Abu Simbel is something of an excursion as it is situated on the edge of Lake Nasser in the desert some 280Km south of Aswan, the nearest main town.

If you are going on a day trip to this site you can be fairly sure that you won't be there for those few minutes when the light is perfect (which would be dawn rather than dusk at this particular site if you do get the chance).

The light during most of the day is harsh and even though the beauty of the carvings is undeniable, it is a shame not to photograph it at its best. There is an alternative, however, which can be seen here with these two photographs.

Both pictures were taken with a Nikon F4S camera and Nikon 75-300mm lens. This allowed me to get the detail of the face of the colossus from the ground at some distance. A smaller lens would have meant that I would have had to get so close to fill the frame with the face, that I would have been looking up at it from an awkward angle. These statues are twenty metres high. If you look closely at the beard of the left-hand photo you will see a bird in flight - that should put it into perspective for you.

So what about the quality of the light? I took the photograph on the right at the same time. I have used an 81C warm-up filter to create this effect. Just as with natural light the sandstone subjects give the most dramatic results. It makes the subject look much warmer and gets around the problem of being at the location at the wrong time of day. It can't be used for every subject because it does have an effect on everything in the shot; blue skies go a little bit brown and anything that is obviously white will just look wrong. With careful use, though, this is an excellent piece of equipment to have in the bag.

Portrait of a photograph

<u>Surma tribal people, Mursi Hana, Omo region of Ethiopia</u>
page 121

This photograph has been published a couple of times but its most prominent use so far has been as the front cover of *Independent & Specialist Travel* magazine.

The main subject is obviously the Surma people, and I was lucky to be able to frame the man, woman and child in one shot. In the background we can see more people talking to Westerners and so the picture sets the scene for the interaction of travellers with locals.

As a cover shot there was enough dead space at the top of the frame to allow the publication title not to spoil the composition, but there were a couple of things that were distracting. The green mug attracts the eye and was neatly cropped from the picture used.

There is also a potential problem with nudity. The publisher was concerned that this could upset the retailers and that he might find his magazine banned from the shelves of W.H.Smiths and John Menzies. In fact the retailers' comments were sought in advance. The potential problem was overcome by placing text over the relevant anatomy - no problem with the bare breast, but for some reason it was deemed provident to place a 'P' over the penis!

I have to admit that whenever I get a photo on a front cover I derive a certain amount of egotistical satisfaction which is often worth more than the financial reward. It is especially pleasing when the magazine is on the shelves of the high street newsagents.

<u>Colours and textures</u>
page 122

Sometimes it is not the obvious subjects that make good photographs. Photography is all about light and colour, so make the most of the medium and look for subjects that catch the light. It is often better to take a close-up detail of something just for the pattern than to stand back and capture the whole scene. These sort of photos are difficult to sell unless you have some particular usage in mind, but that doesn't mean they are useless. Libraries often hold huge stocks of textures and colours which have a very wide potential use in all manner of designs. They are not going to be published on their own, but might, for instance, make stunning backgrounds as part of more complex artwork.

Erg Chebbi, Morocco
page 122

Sand dunes always make a photogenic subject. They can be used as a scenic shot or in close-up for their colour and texture as in the above example.

One problem with them is that they look stunningly beautiful when you are standing looking at them, but once you get the pictures home only you have the advantage of knowing how big they were. You can't tell whether it was a sand heap in a builder's yard, a dune on a beach or a massive desert formation. By taking a shot with people in it the perspective is established. If there aren't any people, there may be wildlife, or a vehicle that you can include in the shot.

As a matter of interest locals claim that Erg Chebbi is the largest dune in the world. It is certainly big and, if nothing else, you could say it is the closest large sand dune to Europe. It therefore gets quite a lot of use as a photographic subject and you probably recognise it from one of the many adverts in which it appears.

Moreno Glacier, Argentina
page 123

This is another example in which scale would have been lost and probably not believed, if the people in the foreground had not been included.

Templo de las Inscripciones, Palenque, Mexico
page 123

I have seen a number of photographs of Mayan pyramids that have been taken from directly in front of the subject. They do make an adequate representation, but it is far better to consider the composition.

Portrait of a photograph

In this photograph I have used a piece of ruined wall to provide some foreground and balance to the right of the frame. Along with the jungle background this helps to give the subject some compositional interest. Again I have used people (at the top of the steps) to give scale.

Inti Raymi at Sacsayhuamán ruins, Peru
page 124

Travellers are usually drawn to the ruins of old civilizations. The sites form the basis of many a tourist route. Unfortunately ruins can make for some very dull photographs, however spectacular the ancient civilizations may have been in their day. If at all possible I like to get some kind of interaction between today's civilizations with the old ruined sites.

This picture is taken at the annual festival of Inti Raymi and I feel the crowds bring the site to life. You can not only see the size and intricacy of the incredible Inca stonework, but also you catch some of the excitement of the festival.

It is always worth checking when local festivals are held and trying to fit in your travel plans around them.

London telephone box
page 124

Anything that is typical of a place is worthy of a photograph. This shot, for example, could only have been taken in London. The signpost has world famous attractions on it such as Buckingham Palace. By framing the shot with plenty of space at the top it allows for text to be overlaid. I took a series of shots of this same phone box with different passers-by in the frame. A shot with a policeman might just say 'London'. A shot with a backpacker walking past might say 'London - a tourist destination', whilst this shot with the Sikhs in frame might say 'London - the cosmopolitan city'. Different people will give the shot different potential uses.

177

Roof of St George's Church, Lalibela, Ethiopia
page 124

This shot has been taken with an ultra wide-angle lens. It has allowed me to fit into the picture the whole of the church roof - the church is cut into the rock itself. Just look at the depth of field - not only can you see the roof in good focus, but there is actually no sky-line in this photograph. At the top of the frame there is a mountain range at a remarkable distance, yet it is still in focus.

The gathered people add atmosphere as well as scale and they help place the picture geographically.

Simien Mountains, Ethiopia
page 157

This is another photograph that was taken with the compact camera, the Samsung ECX1. It was taken during a three day trek into the Simien Mountains National Park. I didn't want to lug all the cameras with me as we had to take all our food, pots and pans and sleeping gear anyway. I just brought along the compact, not realising the sort of spectacular scenery I was about to encounter.

Nevertheless the compact did me proud and I came back with some fantastic shots. This particular shot was used in a magazine as the lead photograph for an article written by a BBC producer who had just made a documentary about a pilgrimage in Ethiopia.

The photograph was noticed by other readers and I received enquiries from picture buyers. This resulted directly in sales of photographs of Ethiopia to two separate companies that were new customers to me.

It just shows the importance of getting your name credited against your pictures. Two new customers without placing an advert, can't be bad.

Portrait of a photograph

Djemaa el Fna, Marrakesh, Morocco
page 158

Whenever the opportunity arises, I try to take photographs from an elevated position. There are very often restaurants, shops or hotels that have a rooftop from which you may get an interesting overview. Simply asking the owners if you can use their roof or window often gets a positive response.

The colours in this shot have been affected by the artificial lighting. The square is well-known for its evening activity and the effect of these lights gives a very atmospheric shot.

The Golden Temple of Amritsar, Punjab, India
page 158

I've mentioned several techniques and subjects for getting a useful, saleable picture. I've put this photo in just to make the point that the main attraction must not be overlooked. There is always a requirement for good shots of the architectural attraction of an area, be they the religious buildings, monuments, ruins or just famous buildings.

This shot is taken at dusk which really shows off the gold of the Golden Temple. Shots from the series have been published several times.

Portraits
page 159

Portraits of people you meet on your travels can make a good subject for a photograph. There is always a temptation to use a long lens and snap away at people in the distance without them knowing about it. You might get some interesting candid street scenes like this, but you will rarely get a good portrait with this technique. It is also a rude infringement of people's privacy. For portraits, your subject needs to be aware of you and happy to pose, smile or ignore your presence so that you can get the photo that you want. Anyone who is the direct subject of a photograph has the right to give or deny their permission.

<u>Dawn over Mitten Buttes, Monument Valley, Arizona, U.S.A.</u>
page 160

If you make a habit of getting up early in the morning to watch the dawn, you will spend many a cold hour waiting, and frequently get disappointing results. There is no guarantee that a dawn shot will be spectacular. Just once in a while, though, a picture like this will come along and make it all worthwhile.

To go to the trouble of getting out of bed, positioning yourself with camera and tripod, and to be rewarded with a dawn like this, knowing you have wherewithal to record it on film, is one of the most satisfying feelings I know.

Chapter 12

The Internet

There is a section of the population that are technophobes and have absolutely no skills in computer-literacy. Technology is moving on at an unbelievable pace regardless of this fact, and moves ahead without them. I realise that many people who would like to get into travel writing and photography are people who spend, or have spent, a considerable amount of their time out of the country, travelling. For someone travelling around the world, especially in developing countries, there is very little chance to keep abreast of the latest developments in the computer age. Some people's travel projects last for years, which is precisely why they feel they have an expert knowledge that would make a good book or some good travel features. The problem is, though, that whilst their travel knowledge excels, technology escapes them.

I cannot go into great depth about the Internet medium but I do firmly believe it's the way of the future, and for many it's already part of everyday life. At this stage it may not be essential, but that does not mean that it will not become so. If you are running a small business as a freelance I think it is well worthwhile keeping up to date and trying to find out about anything that is new and potentially beneficial. If you are working alone, there is no one else that is going to investigate this medium for you. There may or may not be areas of the Internet that can benefit your particular involvement in the business of travel writing and photography, but if you don't look, you won't find out.

At the risk of over-simplifying matters I have written a brief explanation of what you need to get connected to the Internet and the World Wide Web, and the areas which I personally think are of interest.

The hardware you need to get a connection

The first thing you need is a computer with a recommended specification of at least a 486/33MHz with 8MB of RAM. It will work okay with 4MB RAM if you are still using Windows 3.1 rather than the more modern Windows 95.

This processing power requirement is far greater than you would need just to run a simple word processor. It therefore will not be the cheapest thing on the market and might contradict some of the points I raised in chapter 5 about using yesterday's technology for reasons of economy. On the other hand the 486 has largely been out-dated by Pentium processors so could still be considered yesterday's technology.

The next essential is a modem. This is a piece of equipment that converts computer language into a format that can be transmitted down the phone and can similarly de-code incoming information. The faster the capabilities of the modem the quicker the information will be passed and less phone time will be required. Yesterday's modems had a speed of 14,400 bps (bits per second). Today's modems have a speed of at least 28,800 bps and the current fastest are the 33,600 bps - now expressed as 33.6 kbps. Get the best you can afford.

Service Provider

You do not connect directly into the core of Internet computers, but have to gain access via a company that does. These companies are 'Service Providers' and charge you for the facility. The service providers all have their own terms with different services included. Some include free space for your own Web site pages and some provide a certain amount of free connection time. You then pay them extra if you go over the free time. Most have a start-up fee and all have a subscription fee payable either monthly or annually. You will need to research which provider is best for the type of use you expect to get out of the system.

There are occasional offers of a 'free start-up and one month free subscription' to get you started. This is definitely the best way to familiarise yourself with the Internet. You can then decide what you want it for, and re-assess your service provider. Lists of service providers can be found in several computer magazines. Ring up a few providers and see what they have to offer.

Software

You need some software to be able to run the system. This is usually provided free of charge by the Internet Service Provider. If it isn't then think twice about using this provider.

Web Browsers

These are systems that make an attempt to put order into the chaos of the net. They are programs that are either provided in the start-up package or can be obtained from the Internet itself once you have your connection. The most commonly used one is Netscape Navigator although Internet Explorer is hard on its heels and may be a better system.

They allow you to enter certain criteria such as key words and will then go off and search the Web for any matching references. The findings are displayed and you can go straight to the page by pointing and clicking on your choice of the relevant matching reference.

Telephone Line

Your modem needs to be connected to a telephone line to link your computer to the Internet. Whenever you are actually connected, or 'on-line' as the expression is, you are running up a phone bill. This is quite separate and independent from any charges that come from the Service Provider. The phone number you use to connect to the Service Provider will determine the charges you incur from the telephone company. Most Service Providers have local access numbers - numbers that are charged at the rates for a local call.

How we can use it

The Internet is like a massive library. Every writer spends hours researching details for articles so will be quite familiar with libraries. The books in a library, however, have gone through some kind of editing and publishing process that means they have invariably met some standards to enable them to be commercially published. Something found on the Internet has not necessarily undergone any editing process and might therefore be absolute trash and only of interest to the person that wrote it. Somehow you have to wade through all this to find the information that you actually want.

Perhaps the biggest difference between the Internet and a library is the fact that it is interactive; that is to say, you can add your own comments and make direct contact with other individuals whose computers are connected to the network.

You can talk to each other in real time, as with a telephone, or you can leave written messages that people can respond to at their convenience. You can leave messages for a particular individual that only they can retrieve - this is e-mail. You can post a message to a communal Bulletin Board that others can access to leave their replies and comments. You can also set up public conferences where a number of people are connected to each other at the same time and anyone who chooses to connect can join in.

In short, you can have two-way conversations and an exchange of information with any number of people around the world either in real time or by posting and receiving messages at your convenience.

The Internet as a research tool

When you enter a new environment it can be reassuring to find something familiar. The guide book publishers are household names to most travellers, so their Web pages are a good place to start. They have taken an innovative approach to the Internet and provide us with a massive amount of on-line information. It is invaluable when checking facts and researching an article.

Rough Guides led the field, not only producing their own guide 'The Internet & World Wide Web', now in its second edition, but taking the brave step of putting their travel books on-line. They started with their guide to the USA and continued with Canada, Mexico, and Europe guides. Their Australia guidebook is due on-line soon and the rest of their 100 titles will follow in the coming year(s). In the meantime they have brief extracts and summaries of all their guides along with updates from readers.

Their on-line guide to the Web gives links to all manner of useful travel-related Web sites. Their address is: http://www.roughguides.com/

Lonely Planet have an excellent Web site, though they haven't taken the same route as Rough Guides. They have destination guides which give the basics about a country, city or region and they have 'detours' to out of the way places.

There are 'postcard' pages that contain tips sent in by other travellers about various places they have visited.

Their 'On the Road' section has a number of articles sent in by the Lonely Planet writers who are currently out researching the guide books.

They also have 'The Thorn Tree' site which is named after the famous restaurant by that name in Nairobi, where a thorn tree grows through the centre of a restaurant and there is a long tradition of travellers posting notices on a board that is nailed to it. Similarly this Web site is an opportunity for notices to be posted on a travellers' bulletin board.

Lonely Planet have a 'Weblinks' section that rather deftly leads you into a directory of travel-related sites on the Web that they consider to be of most interest. Web address: http://www.lonelyplanet.com.au

I would suggest that the next source of information is the tourist offices from around the world. Most of these have their own Web sites or are at least listed with a contact address and if available, an e-mail address.

Tourism Offices Worldwide Directory are at http://www.mbnet.mb.ca/lucas/travel/

You can get information from the British Foreign and Commonwealth Office who not only have pages of travel advice but also, as a sad reflection on Britain, have a section on 'How you can complain'. If you want to have a look, they are on http://www.fco.gov.uk/

The World Health Organisation has a useful site. They give information on everything from world epidemics to the latest advice about health risks for travellers. They are on http://www.who.ch/

Photography on the Internet

It isn't initially easy to find, but the photo libraries have got together and created a Web site. Have a look at PhotoSource. Here you will find what they claim to be 'the UK's most interesting and informative photographic source'. The Web site consists of lists of the various contributing libraries along with pages for feedback, what's new, a noticeboard and a link to other interesting Web sites (though at present this only lists the British Association of Photo Libraries and Agencies [BAPLA] and 'PHOTON - an electronic magazine on digital photography', but in turn these lead to further information)

It seems to me that this is an excellent way of identifying libraries that you might want to work with, or you may even want to consider setting up your own page and join PhotoSource.

Address: http://www.photosource.cp.uk/photosource

Along similar lines is a company called Picture Search. They operate a 'members only' bulletin board that allows researchers to post their picture requirements and libraries to respond. It's a brilliant idea and it's worth a look at the setup.

They are at http://www.picture-search.demon.cp.uk/

It may or may not be worth joining any of the organisations that have these Web sites. It is a very quick way to spend money and I am not sure, at this stage, whether the returns make it worthwhile. If you are working with a library then these sort of subscriptions are handled by them anyway so perhaps this kind of marketing is best left to them.

The Internet as a publicity tool

The simplest way to publicise yourself on the Internet is to have your own page. A 'Homepage' is a facility that many of the Service Providers offer for free, or at least for quite low costs. You can say who you are and what you do and link your e-mail contact address into the page. You can put in a few articles to make it interesting and as a sample of your work and can offer articles for publication that could potentially catch an editor's eye.

Taking part in forums and conferences as an expert in your particular travel topic will also get your name about. Gradually, more of the travelling public are coming on-line and these people are your potential readers - indirectly they are your market for travel writing and photography as they will also be the ones who read the travel pages of newspapers and magazines.

This seems to me to be a natural extension of the points I made in chapter 8 about getting yourself known.

Overall I think that the potential of the Internet is quite overwhelming. I haven't directed you to many Web sites because once you get into one you will quite naturally be led on to the others that you find of interest. There is a danger of overspending on this medium both in terms of the hardware that would make it easier to use, and the time spent on-line, incurring phone bills and possibly on-line charges from your service provider. There is so much else to spend money on to get this business set up that I think equipping yourself with an Internet link is low on the list of priorities. Don't forget that there are Cyber cafés where you can use the net without owning all the kit. This may be a cheap option if you happen to have one within striking distance of your home.

Chapter 13

What the professionals say

Over the course of this book I have explained many of the ins and outs of the travel writing and photography business. I have identified all the things that were totally new to me when I first started in the industry a few years ago. I do not claim to be anywhere near the top of the heap and certainly think that I have a great deal more to learn. There have been several areas which I felt I could not really get to grips with until I learned by trial and error and there are no instant short cuts into the industry. Certainly it is difficult to find good advice from people who are actually doing the job as they are usually far too busy to take time out to speak to everyone who wants to get into the business.

I realise, however, that my own views are not necessarily the right or wrong way of going about things, rather they are just observations of what I perceive to be the way to make the industry pay for me.

Accepting my own limitations of experience, I have taken this final chapter to ask the professionals what they think about getting into the industry. Their views are only really relevant to their particular experience or their particular publication. Taken together, however, it adds up to a fairly comprehensive view from the top. There are a number of common points that are raised in the interviews as well as some that are specific to the individual interviewee, rather than being general for the trade. None of the comments, however, should be ignored.

Lyn Hughes - Wanderlust Magazine

Lyn Hughes is the editor of Wanderlust Magazine. As the magazine's name suggests, it is very much aimed at travellers and sets out to 'inspire the free-spirited traveller'. As a very high profile publication with superb photos and editorials, it provides the ideal market for any travel writer and photographer. I spoke to Lyn to get some tips and points of view from her, and to find out what she wants from her potential contributors.

"Lyn, I remember you told me that at one point you were getting so many submissions sent in that statistically only one in 700 was getting published. Is this still the case?"

"We are getting slightly less than we used to, but we are getting more proposals than finished articles. This is good; if somebody whose work I don't know sends in a nice proposal, I will try to write an encouraging letter back. It stops people wasting their time if they enquire first with a letter or a proposal. Don't necessarily phone up the editor because you probably won't be put through, but there might be somebody else in the editorial office that people can speak to just to find out if something has been run or not.

We are still getting more submissions than I can read, so we still get backlogs, but it's not as bad as it was. We are getting a much higher proportion from people who have read our guidelines and who have read the magazine, which is very encouraging. We are not getting so many of the people who haven't got a clue, who I haven't got a lot of time for."

"Do you think that because Wanderlust is becoming recognised for its quality and style that some unpublished potential contributors are being put off, thinking they have no chance of getting things into your magazine?"

"There might be a certain degree of that. Because we are aware that our readers are very keen travellers and have some very good stories to tell, we have introduced the *Traveller's Tales* section. The idea is that we will be running about three such tales in each issue. I think it's a nice way for somebody who hasn't necessarily been published before, as well as for professional writers, to contribute to the magazine. I would suggest to anybody who is at the first step and wants to put their toe in the water, that they should perhaps try something like this first."

"And do they get paid the same rates for this?"

"Yes they do. They get treated in exactly the same way as any of our other travel writers."

"Having managed to get your attention and perhaps to get a traveller's tale into Wanderlust, what is the key to continuing to write, rather than it being a one-off thing?"

"Professionalism is so important," she told me. "There have been a couple of times when people have very badly missed their deadlines when they have been commissioned to do something. Obviously we don't use them again and we make sure that other editors know about it. Once you have got a foot in the door somewhere, if you do get a commission you have got to fulfil it. Otherwise you won't get a second chance. You have got to meet deadlines and you have got to meet the length that is asked for."

"Do you think that is one of the most important things you are looking for from a contributor?"

"Yes, professionalism. That doesn't mean that you have to be a professional. If I am sent a piece that is good enough to use but the author didn't seem very professional, then obviously I wouldn't take the risk on commissioning a second piece from them. I need to be convinced that a writer would actually be up to taking on a commission."

"Do you get a lot of submissions that you throw out straight away because they're not presented correctly?"

"We do have our own guidelines for contributors and that does actually help a lot. It tells people how to present an article and what we are looking for."

"But presumably there are those who send things in without having asked for your guidelines."

"Oh, yes. I still get hand-written pieces sent in occasionally, which I just don't consider at all, they have to go straight back.

We occasionally get people's diaries. When someone has written a diary on their trip, they literally send in the whole diary and say 'All my friends and family have read the diary and told me how wonderful it is. I thought you might like to take some extracts from it'.

Sometimes we get people at the other extreme who are obviously into desk top publishing. They actually send in a finished piece, laid out as they would lay it out in a magazine. This is their format and they will even put notes at the bottom saying 'this is my suggested format but if you feel it should be different can we please discuss that'," she laughed as she told me.

"Do you see that as a catchy way of doing things or does that just make you laugh and send it back?"

"No, I don't think it has any great benefit. No, frankly."

"You don't think they have taken the trouble to really look at the way you do things and tried to present it the way you want it?" I could tell from Lyn's tone that this was definitely a "no" but I wondered just what she had been presented with.

"Perhaps if it really did look like a Wanderlust article, I would think that. If they had put in all the things that we do I would have thought 'Oh yes, that's clever'. But they don't."

"What about photographs? Do you think it helps sell the article if you can present a package?"

"I think it's wonderful if you can, particularly if you are doing an obscure destination, or if you are talking about something, somewhere, or some people in a very specific way. If you're talking about some remote village in Outer Mongolia, we aren't going to find pictures anywhere else. In that case pictures become almost essential and it will definitely sell it. In a more marginal case, if you can supply the photos it is a great help and there have certainly been articles where we have asked to see the photographs because we know that will help to sway our decision on whether we use the article or not. But having said that, the majority of articles we use these days we do look for photographs elsewhere as well. It would be unlikely that we would turn down an article just because the author hadn't got photographs.

It is a great advantage for the author if they can take the photographs as well, because they are going to get a lot more money from us. And of course it is making it easier for the editor. So complete packages are nice, but we don't expect them. Frankly I don't think there are that many people who can write and take photographs to a high enough standard, particularly if they have been on a fairly short trip. It might be different if they have spent a long time somewhere or if they have visited the place several times. To have gone somewhere for a week or two I think it is very difficult to come back with a complete package."

"What about the Internet; do you get anything coming through to you electronically?"

"I'm being very cautious about the Internet. I already get between 50 and 100 items of conventional mail per day and I don't want to be deluged with letters, junk mail and wannabe writers. I just think it will increase my workload, particularly as it would give more overseas people a link to us. Perhaps in the future I may be prepared to take finished articles from commissioned writers over the Internet, but I don't want unsolicited articles coming through the net. I think it will just clog it all up."

"Do you use the net yourself for information?"

"Yes. I use it for destination sites and there are sites intended for travel agents which are packed full of useful information. It is extremely useful for fact checking - I think it has got a role for things like that. It will be useful for getting small snippets of information such as time-tables. If you are sitting in your office and want to know what time the ferries go on Lake Victoria you can look them up on the net.

I get very upset if I find a fact that I've printed has been incorrect. Our readers are active travellers which is why they get the magazine. Any mis-information in there does get picked up. They know about it, and we get abusive letters and phone calls. Of course it is all our fault. I can see where they are coming from. They are experienced travellers and they rely on having good, up-to-date and correct information."

"Can you summarise your advice for somebody trying to get into the business?"

"I do think it is important that people think laterally. Particularly when you are just starting up, instead of just thinking about the travel sections of the national newspapers and the obvious places like

Wanderlust, you have got to think about all the other magazines and newspapers, regional newspapers, local newspapers, newsletters and all sorts of other things out there. There are lots of opportunities. It's incredible how many magazines these days that you think have no obvious link to travel actually put a travel section in. It is such a popular topic now.

You also have to think laterally about topics and angles. Think laterally, and even try to see if you can get a little regular spot in something - just doing a small piece on a regular basis."

A tremendous amount of information can be gleaned from this one conversation. Remember that these comments come from a magazine editor who actually buys articles and photographs. For we writers and photographers the magazine is the potential customer and we are being given an insight into what the customer wants. It is quite gratifying to see that many of the points Lyn Hughes raised confirm the points I have been trying to get across in this book.

She tells us how to approach an editor, the need for professionalism without having to be a professional, the importance of presentation, how not to approach and present things, the fact that photos can not only increase your income but at times can actually sell the piece. She accepts that the internet is a good source of up-to-date research information, expounds the need to have some angle, something different, and most importantly the need to get published absolutely anywhere to get things started. I am convinced that these are some of the most important lessons to be learnt when breaking into the business and that following any of this advice is taking the right steps that need to be taken to make it pay.

Simon Calder - The Independent

Simon Calder is the travel correspondent and travel editor for The Independent. Obviously every editor is looking for a different product and Simon's stance is quite different from that of Lyn Hughes. Pictures don't seem to be a big seller, nor is there much chance of making money out of The Independent. Having said that, it is interesting to see how Simon himself has managed to turn his own travel writing into a very successful career which clearly does allow him to make a living from The Independent.

I knew that Simon Calder had not always been a travel writer and tried to find out which paths he had taken, and what had been his driving force.

"All I've ever wanted to do was to travel and so it wasn't a question of setting out wanting to write, it was just a matter of finding something which enabled me to travel more," he told me.

This, I suspect, is the motivation for most of us. Travel is the burning ambition, but that doesn't automatically give us the ability to write. Even if we can write there is no guarantee of making a success of it. I wanted to know more about the process of achieving these heights.

"How did you manage to get into the position you are in now?" I asked Simon.

"Oh gosh...," there was a brief pause while he considered the matter. "I suppose only by starting off in a small way and just writing more and more. But it's not something which I ever sought, so 'by accident' I would say is the answer to that".

It just shows that there are no set routes to plot your way into this industry if the travel editor of a major national newspaper has managed to get there "by accident".

"I was just doing odd bits and pieces for The Independent which suited them, because I tended to go to places they wouldn't have that many stories from, and also I fitted in with the policy of not taking anything based on free trips," he continued.

"So were you aiming for The Independent all the time?"

"No, I wasn't aiming for anybody. It just worked out that way, but in terms of actually going out and selling things I was lousy, I think. Because I never tried."

"So you were lucky; being able to write the right thing for the right people at the right time".

"Well, no. No, I wouldn't claim that. It began by me going off to places and saying 'do you want anything?' and it developed from that. Before I got this job I would say 'I'm thinking of doing this trip. If I were to do that would you be interested in this piece or that piece?' and I would take it to the paper. But it had to be done entirely on the basis that The Independent doesn't actually ever commission work."

"And is that still a good approach for The Independent today?"

"Well The Independent has less money than any other paper I would say, so as a writer you have to be prepared to invest a lot, and take knockbacks. I think the key is never ever to have to depend on it, because it is such an uncertain business. I was working as an engineer some of the time and that was keeping body and soul together.

Obviously in terms of The Independent, you have to have another means of survival because we don't pay very well and we don't take any free trips."

This is indeed quite a drawback when you look at the fees paid by The Independent. They pay about £170 per thousand words, but many of the articles they accept are only about 800 words long. You aren't going to get very fat on 136 quid, especially if you personally have had to pay for all the travel. Every angle has to be covered to make this job pay and if you are lucky enough to be getting free trips that exclude you from this particular publication, it must mean that you already have some fairly worthwhile contacts. Whatever your circumstances it would be unwise to ignore The Independent as a potential outlet. There will always be times when you do fit in with their requirements. After all, even regular travel writers who get free trips frequently are always going to go on holiday or self fund a trip at some stage. Perhaps these holidays are the opportunities to write something for The Independent.

Thinking more broadly about increasing the profitability from this market I went on to ask Simon about the potential of increased sales from including photographs. The answer on this particular occasion, I have to admit, was disappointing.

"Do you think it helps if people can offer a package, offering photographs along with the written piece?"

"No. Actually it's completely the reverse. We are very much focused on words. If the words aren't any good then that's the end of the story. Not being picture-led we do not have the facilities for looking after huge numbers of pictures. So if people want to get a swift rejection probably the best way to do it is to send in pictures. There is nothing worse, as I'm sure you will appreciate, than, if you've got a busy desk, people sending you in pictures that you just do not want to use".

"What about sending in laser prints with the article, then it doesn't matter so much if they get lost?"

"Well that's OK, but I'm sorry, I like a fax; only because that means I can make a quick decision and it's not something which necessarily needs to be sent back."

Moving away from the nitty-gritty of getting things into The Independent, Simon did have some advice for newcomers who seriously want to get into travel writing. He recommended that they should consider writing a guidebook. Having put a considerable amount of time and effort into guides on Cuba, he can comment on this genre with authority.

"The discipline," he explained "is a very valuable lesson to be learnt. No one could call early mornings spent checking out budget hotels and train time-tables a lot of fun, but it has to be done. Anybody who finds travel writing easy isn't doing it right. To know how to do this research is just as important when you are writing an article as a guide.

Of course I appreciate that there is a huge difference between writing a guide book and writing an article. In a guide people want useful and up-to-date information because they are intending to visit a place. Many people who read an article have absolutely no intention of ever going to the destination so it is of little interest to them how many budget hotels there are. They want to read something interesting about the place. I do think, though, that if you are seriously trying to get into travel writing, guide books are a good way of learning the trade."

Well there we have it; we're given some advice on how you might break into the industry and also promised that faxes will bring quick decisions from The Independent. There is no point in them approaching with ideas based on free trips and there is an in-built expectation that you will not make a living from the writing alone.

So I drew a blank on the photos, but that's not the end of the world. The important thing with any of these markets is to know what the buyer is looking for. If he doesn't want photos, make sure you only send him the very best of your words that stand up on their own without the need for illustration. The trip, whatever it might have been, will undoubtedly have yielded some photos but this isn't the place to offer them. We need to look for a photo-led market for them. Perhaps there is an opportunity to sell some words to The Independent, some photos to a travel brochure and a words-and-photo feature to a magazine. Use all the markets to make it pay.

Nicholas Crane - Travel writer and broadcaster

Nicholas Crane successfully makes his living from travel writing. He is the author of five travel books and co-author of a further three. He is a frequent contributor to the Daily and Sunday Telegraph. He has made two films for television and three radio documentaries for Radio 4. His most recent book *Clear Waters Rising* has just been published by Viking Penguin and recounts an epic mountain walk across Europe.

As a freelance writer with a track record such as this, Nicholas is clearly making money from several different areas of travel writing. I wanted to know if writing travel books makes money. I asked him whether he thought that if a newcomer set out to write just travel books, rather than also writing articles, it would be possible to make a living from it.

"Not under the method I used, no," was his honest reply. "The book which has just been published, *Clear Waters Rising*, took me two and a half years to write and the journey itself lasted one and a half years. So it has been a four-year full-time project. I suppose if I costed it out I was being paid about a penny an hour.

You have got to be extremely passionate to write books. You've got to want to do it more than anything else - more than earning a living. It's a masochistic kind of occupation - I love it! But I've never been able to do it without propping it up with journalism."

I wondered if journalism, and particularly his work for the Telegraph, had been his door into the industry, but I soon found out that this was not the case.

"I always wanted to write and started writing stories for the fun of it when I was a teenager. It wasn't until I was in my twenties that I realised there was a possibility of actually earning a living from it. My first ever travel article was a piece on cycle camping for *She* magazine. I got into travel writing by writing a guide book in 1979 which very fortunately went into Penguin paperback almost immediately. That was a stroke of luck - and was what got me going."

It was interesting to hear yet again that guide book writing formed a foundation for a career in travel writing. I was rather taken with the idea of a stroke of luck as well, because I'm sure we all need some of that. Luck alone was not enough though, and Nicholas' career was based on a great deal of hard work and thoroughly immersing himself in the industry.

"For the first five years I did a part-time editing job as well, commissioning other writers and photographers, writing copy, dealing with printers and so on for a book publisher. It taught me a lot about the industry and about photography. So I have had a background in the other end of the production line, which is very helpful."

"Was that really your bread and butter while you were getting the freelance writing going?" I asked him.

"It was, but within the editing job I was writing thousands of words every month for a yearbook, and I was writing regularly for various magazines at that time. I didn't begin writing for broadsheet newspapers until about 1985."

"Do you think starting with magazines is better than going for the broadsheets?"

"No, I think there is no rule. It happens to have been the route I took. The broadsheets are regarded by many as being the pinnacle of journalistic achievement. The standards are more rigorous than any other type of journal in the UK, and they are the most difficult to get into. Paradoxically they are often not the best paid. If you are aiming for a journal or a newspaper with high standards then it inevitably pushes your own standards up."

"If you were just trying to get into the business nowadays, what do you think a newcomer should aim for?"

"If there is a rule, it is to ignore the rules and to follow your own nose. One of the benefits of following your own enthusiasms is that it shows in your writing. Stick to subjects that you really feel close to and highly motivated to work on, because without that motivation and enthusiasm you won't be able to persuade editors to go for it."

Certainly the idea of following my own nose and my own enthusiasm appeals and I think that most people who are seriously considering travel writing and photography will be the kind of people that have little time for conventions and rules. Most of the money, however, is in the hands of people with commercial interests and they generally have a problem with the unconventional. It doesn't make it easy to find funding for new and exciting trips, as Nicholas explains.

"If I'm sufficiently fired up by the uniqueness and originality of a trip or expedition, I haven't got the patience to drag other people like financial sponsors along with me. By nature my trips are always green trips; they are low-tech and have a minimal environmental footprint. They need no backup and support. By definition they are extremely low budget; in fact I think that almost all of my trips have been so low budget that they have been less expensive than staying in my own home.

I don't like my trips to have any strings attached. I want to be able to do my own thing and I don't want the obligation of promoting somebody's anorak when I get back. I don't want to be beholden to anybody.

On my last trip, the year and a half mountain walk across Europe, I hadn't spoken to publishers before I set off, had no publishing deal, and I didn't even have a solid newspaper tie-up. Most people thought I wouldn't succeed or they couldn't grasp its scale. It was too big for them to pick up on it. It wasn't until I had set off and was totally out of contact with the UK that people started noticing, which is very often the case with big trips."

I was quite surprised by this and would have thought that an established writer like Nicholas Crane would have had no trouble in drumming up interest in his projects or in finding sponsorship. It certainly shows that you don't have to be chasing every penny with premeditated commercialism. If you are confident in your abilities you can fund your own trips and sell the product after the journey.

"What was it like trying to sell the book when you got back?" I asked him.

"It went fairly crazy. I have a literary agent and he held an auction. I think there were about ten or twelve publishers bidding for it, so it went very successfully."

"Do you think people trying to write books need to have an agent?"

"I think it helps, yes."

"Presumably you were able to get an agent because you were already an established writer."

"No, I got my agent when I'd had two books published, but they were both guide books. They were hardly what I would call main-stream publishing and they were hardly promising material for any agent to get involved in. So I would say that I got my agent before I was properly established as an author."

I'm not entirely sure that you could call someone with two books to their name an unestablished writer, especially when the first of those books was taken up by Penguin paperbacks. Perhaps this is just a matter of modesty, but I must say that I have never actually tried to get an agent so can't really comment with any authority.

I also wanted to know what Nicholas thought about photography. He lists himself as a writer and broadcaster with no mention of photography. Is this modesty again, doesn't he take photos, or is it just part of his productivity that he takes for granted?

"I regard myself as being an old-fashioned photo-journalist," he told me. "I come back with a story and a picture to go with it. I do all my own photography, both for my books and my newspaper writing. So I provide my own photographs for the Daily Telegraph and the Sunday Telegraph."

"And do you find that a big help?"

"Well yes," he seemed surprised at my question, "you earn a lot more money! It is extremely hard work though. If I am on an assignment with a limited timescale, typically I will be working from 6 am to 12 pm. Photography is nearly always best done at dawn and dusk and then you have got to do all the interviews to get the material for the copy and so on. It is as far removed from going on a holiday as flying to the moon is from going on a country walk. You really have to focus on objectives and be extremely selective and thorough, quite analytical about what it is you are looking for.

I'm not complaining - I mean, it *is* great fun."

"Is it still as much of a struggle to get a commission as it ever was?"

"I think once you have been writing for a newspaper for a few years then it does get easier, but you are only as good as your last piece. If you start handing in duff pieces you won't get any more work.

I have always felt that travel writing has been a meritocracy. If you come up with a good idea and it's well-written then it ought to get published. There is a hunger for column inches."

Nicholas had one final piece of advice for anyone trying to make a living out of travel writing and photography which I think confirms one of the main points I have been putting forward over the course of this book.

"I think diversity is the key to survival," he said. "If you are a competent writer and photographer - and you can find a way into radio and TV too - then it widens the scope for survival."

Hilary Bradt - Bradt Publications

Hilary Bradt is a travel writer who is perhaps best known as the founder of Bradt Publications, which publishes a series of well respected travel guides - the Bradt Guides.

The comments from Simon Calder and Nicholas Crane brought out the fact that many travel writers have a guide book somewhere in their CV. I wanted to find out if a guide book publisher saw their medium as a training ground for new writers. I spoke to Hilary Bradt and she certainly didn't want to encourage every would-be writer to go out and learn their trade at the publisher's expense. Having said that, she recognised that many guide book authors were subsequently going on to write articles for newspapers and magazines.

"When people write to me and say 'I haven't written anything before but I'd really like to write a guide book,' my heart sinks," she warned me. "We publish good writing, which I think is as important in a guide book as the facts."

She went on to explain her reasons which, of course, make fine commercial sense. It wasn't all bad news for the newcomer, though. She was quick to add that she was not necessarily looking for established professionals, just good and enthusiastic writers.

"I want someone who can write well," she explained. "That way I'm not spending a huge amount of the book's budget on editing them. It is not that somebody needs to be a published writer, but I do always ask to see a sample of their writing."

So if people didn't have to be published writers how were they to convince her that they were good writers, and more to the point how would they convince themselves?

"If you're a good writer you're going to know it anyway because you will have a strong desire to express yourself in writing. You will write letters because you can't help yourself. When you experience a place you have to put it into words.

A real writer isn't inspired by commercialism, they want to tell someone about a place and most people have friends or family that they want to write to. They develop their travel writing skills by writing letters home when they do their early trips."

"I am not suggesting that you take all and sundry and dump them on the guide book publishers to learn their trade," I assured Hilary, "but I have noticed that several of the writers that are well up in the profession have themselves written guide books at some stage."

"That is a good way of putting it," Hilary admitted. "I get so many letters from people that aren't suitable as writers, I would just hate people to think 'Oh, I'll get my training writing some guide books'. But what you say is completely true. As we speak I'm writing a guide book myself and I have honed my writing skills..." she paused a minute. "You are leading me into your opinion exactly because, in fact, I now write travel articles, having got my skills writing travel guides. However I published the guides myself so it wasn't at the expense of any other publisher!"

"How do you actually go about recruiting authors for your books?"

"Too many writers go down the lists in the *Writers' and Artists' Yearbook* and write to everyone who has the word 'travel' in the listing," she told me.

"Yes, I've done that," I said, making myself look foolish. She laughed politely, probably hoping I was joking.

"A good potential author," she continued, "will go to somewhere like Stanfords and will look at books and become familiar with them. Hopefully they will even use them when they are travelling and will know which publisher appeals to them the most. A Lonely Planet author isn't necessarily a Bradt author. There are different approaches. The ones that impress me are the ones that are familiar with the Bradt Guides. I have enough people coming to me so that generally I don't have to recruit. If the enthusiasm is really there someone will seek me out, but I am very busy, I only publish six new titles a year, and I can't cope with too much choice."

Well, enthusiasm seems to be the key yet again. All indications have been that travel writing won't earn you a fortune, especially in the early days. Perhaps Hilary had a different view of this; was guide book writing to be the secret to a fortune? I know she had already said that writers aren't motivated by money but we do all need to keep body and soul together. The question just had to be asked:

"Do they make money out of it, Hilary?" I put it bluntly.

"Not much," she admitted light-heartedly. "Well actually, that's not true. I work on a system where I give a low advance, but reasonable royalties. We have to be sharing the risk equally between the author and publisher. If a book does well, we both do well. If it does badly, we both do badly. This does mean that it is hard for first-time authors who have to mainly finance their own trip. Someone who writes for me and is getting into third and fourth editions does fine, because the updating is nowhere near as expensive as the initial book, nor does it take as much time, but he or she still gets the same royalty. For first-time people it is difficult. Perhaps it means that those who are really enthusiastic and committed will still do the book and I think that is why I have such good authors.

There are a couple of writers that make a living out of Bradt Guides.

Both of them have used it as a spring-board, getting articles published that they wouldn't previously have had accepted. They are now established travel writers for magazines and newspapers.

The payments for articles is better and quicker and I think it is almost an essential backup to guide book writing."

It is interesting to learn that not all guide book publishers go about things in the same way. In chapter 3 (page 43), I mentioned the arrangements offered by Rough Guides, and indeed Pat Yale gave us some of the details about contracts with Lonely Planet and contracts she had turned down.

Moving away from the specific business of guide books I went on to find out if Hilary had any advice for newcomers in general. Remember that Hilary doesn't only write guides, she is also an established article writer and gets her work published in prestigious publications like The Times, The Telegraph and The Independent, along with a number of magazines.

"Yes, looking at the industry both as a writer and as a publisher, I think it is essential to get the query letter right; you can spoil your chances forever by getting it wrong. I cannot emphasise enough the importance of spelling correctly, and getting the publisher's name right. I once rejected a very well-established author who also had a good idea for a book, which I would have liked to do. It was such a shame, but I had to write to him and say that 'because you have spelt my name three different ways in one letter, I don't think that you would have the accuracy required for the task'. If they can't get things right in a query letter I won't accept it even if I like the proposal. And I am impressed by good headed paper, it's all the little sort of frills that people nowadays think aren't necessary. I've got a right to be old-fashioned; I know what I want."

If Hilary knows what she likes to receive she will obviously make sure that her own work goes out in a suitable way. I think it is always worth putting yourself in the place of an editor receiving your work and trying to imagine what your first impressions would be. Chapter 7 deals with the issue of presentation in some length.

Her final point is an issue that several people are quite negative about. It is a subject, I might add, that is extremely pertinent to this book, although I have not covered the topic in these pages.

"Self-publishing," she reminded me, "is how we all started - how the Wheelers started (Lonely Planet), how Bill Dalton started (Moon Publications) and how I started. There are people who do well with this, even in the travel narrative side, which is what everybody wants to do. People don't actually want to write guide books; they want to write the story of their trip. There are plenty of people who have done an excellent trip and who can write well about it, but it hasn't got that something that will get a mainstream publisher taking it. It is jolly hard to get even a good book published. It's a real shame, it's all to do with gimmicks and names. If you are a film star or whatever, you don't have to write very well, and it will get published. You will get published if you are an outstanding writer, but if you are just a good writer who has done a good trip you won't. You've either got to have a gimmick in the trip or you have got to be famous. I think self-publishing is a really sensible option, but you need some way of selling the books, such as giving travel lectures."

In conclusion

It seems to me that there is absolutely no point in trying to take on this way of life if you can't write or take photographs in the first place. You simply won't succeed if you approach things the wrong way but there are certainly opportunities for those who approach things the right way.

Hilary commented to me that she considers her approach to the business as 'idiosyncratic' - but then isn't everyone's? That is precisely why we need to assimilate different points of view. My own points of view that I have expressed throughout this book are just one way of looking at the industry. If you have read this, and intend to make a living out of travel writing and photography, you are now equipped with all you need to know to make it pay. The matter of individual style and specific approach, however, is still down to you. There is a lot of food for thought in what the four professionals - Lyn Hughes, Simon Calder, Nicholas Crane and Hilary Bradt - have told us. Much of it corroborates what I have written in these pages.

USEFUL ADDRESSES

ARTS COUNCIL OF ENGLAND
14 Great Peter Street, London SW1P 3NQ
Tel: 0171 333 0100

BRITISH ASSOCIATION OF PICTURE LIBRARIES AND AGENCIES (BAPLA)
18 Vine Hill, London EC1R 5DX
Tel: 0171 713 1780. Fax: 0171 713 1211

BRITISH GUILD OF TRAVEL WRITERS (BGTW)
Secretary: John Harrison
90 Corringway, London W5 3HA
Tel: 0181 998 2223

BRITISH INSTITUTE OF PROFESSIONAL PHOTOGRAPHY
Amwell End, Ware, Hertfordshire SG12 9HN
Tel: 01920 464011 Fax: 01920 487056

BUREAU OF FREELANCE PHOTOGRAPHERS
Focus House, 497 Green Lanes, London N13 4BP
Tel: 0181 882 3315 Fax: 0181 886 5174

NATIONAL UNION OF JOURNALISTS (NUJ)
Acorn House, 314 Gray's Inn Road, London WC1X 8DP
Tel: 0171 278 7916 Fax: 0171 837 8143

THE ROYAL PHOTOGRAPHIC SOCIETY
The Octagon, Milsom Street, Bath BA1 1DN
Tel: 01225 462841 Fax: 01225 448688

THE SOCIETY OF AUTHORS
84 Drayton Gardens, London SW10 9SB
Tel: 0171 373 6642

Quick reference index

All you need to know about: